TODAY'S
SURVIVAL GUIDE
Psalms, Proverbs, Ecclesiastes

DR. STEPHEN HARRISON
AND RICHARD HUIZINGA

Integrity Publishing
39343 Harbor Hills Blvd Lady Lake,
FL 32159

www.integrity-publishing.com

CONTETNS

PREFACE

Scholars cannot say with a great deal of certainty that any particular author wrote a particular book in the Bible. Indeed, more often there is more convincing evidence that an acclaimed author did not write a book. That hardly takes away the meaning of such a work. Indeed, the appeal to some connection by using a name is meant to enhance the meaning and significance of a work. Consider the Books of Moses or the Gospels and supposed connection to the disciples, etc. No less considerations may be at play with Psalms, Proverbs, and Ecclesiastes.

Do the Psalms have less impact if king David did not write them? Even the 23rd psalm? Do we have a different understanding of King David if he did not write the 23rd Psalm? Do we have a different appreciation of psalm 23 if David did not write this? By the same token many have attributed Proverbs to King Solomon and Ecclesiastes as well. Does the authorship of these works matter for the ultimate meaning in our life? Our goal when we set out to write from the heart of the Bible with these three books was to find the heart of the meaning and not the heart of any given individual.

We have attempted to find the heart of David in our book entitled David and Michelangelo Heart and Stone. Finding the heart of David, who is said to be after the heart of God can be an elusive exercise. Ultimately to do so we must remove our preconceptions both of David and perhaps God. Our ask in this work is that you also remove your preconceptions of authorship and individuals. We ask that you enter this work with the mind of a child which is akin to the beginner mind in Zen.

Nonetheless, we do recognize that there may be some benefit in trying to make connections for authorship. Having a name in mind may make the literature more meaningful in many instances by helping us to make a connection with some other important event. Ultimately, the individual must assign their own meaning to any given work. The final arbiter for finding meaning in any work comes in its application in our daily lives as we maintained in our book Parables and Paradox. It is our profound hope that the reader come to the heart of the Bible and find meaning in their heart and life that they may apply on a daily basis.

INTRODUCTION

Survival Skills

Salvation at Another Level

Growing up, going to church was a weekly Sunday morning necessity. And as I remember it, the reading of the Law, the Ten Commandments were the first order of worship. Sometimes, we received a treat and only heard the Summary of the Law. Regardless, whether complete or a summary, the Law was a serious matter and required reverent listening and follow up action. Although as a youngster I wasn't quite sure how to do some of the actions God seemed to be calling for.

As I grew a little older, the Summary of the Law seemed to make more sense and I could understand its meaning in everyday life. The meaning of the Ten Commandments and its archaic language had been lost on a youngster's mind. The Summary of the Law was a little less daunting: Thou shalt love the Lord your God with all you heart, soul and mind. The second part is like unto it: Do unto others as you would have them do unto you.

Still, "The Law", The Ten Commandments and the follow-on Torah of Biblical and current times seemed to be a dark and deadly force meant to foster behavior that would please a Powerful God and keep everyone in line whether they wanted to or not. Deviate from the Law and you were cloaked in Sin, or at best you would not feel worthy or righteous or "good". In fact, even as an adult, many of us feel that living under The Law is a burden and a ponderous weight to keep us buttoned down and controlled. Yet, there are other opinions and lifestyles that come into play. For instance, David, who knew the Law well and wrote this response in Psalm 119:

> Direct me to the path of your commands, for there I find delight.
> Turn my heart toward your Laws and away from selfish gain.

> David in Psalm 119, turns both The Law and its Summary around and replies to God, in effect saying:

> "You know God, you're right!"

> "I see that these weren't Commands just to make you happy, or me miserable, they were commands and laws to help, to please me and help me serve others."

We may have viewed the Law as a downer, but God didn't. And neither did David. A Similar confirming message of God's intentions was delivered by God in Jeremiah: I have plans for you, to Prosper you and to Bless you.

My Summary: On this side of Eternity, it looks like God is trying to save us from ourselves; to survive.

PSALMS

INTRODUCTION

Survival Skills

Psalm 1, Psalm 119, Proverbs and Ecclesiastes, form the basis of a guide to survive many of the evil and ill-advised onslaughts of this world as well as a pathway to achieve personal and social salvation. The advice and direction offered by these Old Testament books are relevant to today's culture and challenges, despite their antiquity, simply because today's motivations for evil and virtue are the same as biblical times, a fact known by God when He provided them to those ancient cultures. God offered them then, and offers them now, simply because Gods advice, motivation and direction have no expiration date.

Psalm 1 offers its advice in a pertinent, direct and straight forward manner focusing on two options: the court of the righteous and the court of the wicked. We also get the consequences of each choice. For example: Focus on and choose the court of the righteous, then the result is: you will flourish and prosper. Choose the court of the wicked and the result is: That you will wither and be driven away from the Lord only to be forever unsettled.

The Psalm's observation to Meditate on the Word Day and Night definitely implies to be serious about it and to make our meditation a daily, a regular practice. Interestingly, an ancient English writer translates the word Meditates as the verb Exercises. To me, that means we not only take our time in the Word seriously, but be constantly searching for the deeper and personal meaning that God meant for us to discover in His Word.

Rich

INTRODUCTION TO PSALMS

When we think of the Psalms we naturally think of David. He is after all, given credit for writing a high percentage of them. Whether or not that is historically accurate is not the purpose of this treatise. Rather we believe that we demonstrate here a style in the Psalms that is consistent from the image that we have come to understand that is the David that we portrayed in our book David and Michelangelo: Heart and Stone. That portrayal is taken directly from the scripture and contains a number of elements that are often ignored or suppressed.

We find in the Psalms, like the other scriptures, the David we are willing to see. We will certainly find the familiar Psalms and familiar platitudes. We take great comfort in these whether it is Psalm 23 or other familiar psalms. We wish to find peace and comfort. We wish to appreciate nature. We also have moments when we wish to see the majesty of creation and offer praise to the creator. We expect along the way to see a little sectionalism where the people of that creator God will be favored over other people.

Yet if we continue to look, we will see additional elements that may not be so comforting or so full of praise. We might return to the 23rd Psalm to catch a potential glimpse of additional perspectives. We see the humble shepherd background that represents the bridge between nature, occupation, and his role for God's people. Of course, Christianity extends this to the role of Christ and extends other analogies and comparisons. We see here that God is guiding David in the path of righteousness for God's name sake.

David likes to emphasize throughout the Psalms that God has an opportunity to defend God's good name and his people by helping David out. Indeed, that opportunity comes with an obligation that you will see throughout the Psalms. David will flat out tell God what to do at times. We then see that David will expect God to respond and then claim that David is blessed because he follows the correct pathway as is suggested here. In Psalm 23 David portrays no fear because he walks a righteous path. This is not the David of many other psalms where he fears for his own life. Unless, of course, that God will rescue him.

Even in our beloved psalm we see the ever-taunting David. He taunted Goliath on the battlefield. He taunted all of the Philistines. Arguably he taunts men whose partners that he desires only to later sometimes taunt his own partners. We find a brief reference to that in the 23rd psalm where he notes that there is a table prepared in the presence of his enemies. He is anointed for all to see including his enemies. David uses some positive self-talk when he says that surely goodness and love will follow him all of his life.

This brings us to the final perspective we wish to highlight in this introduction of the Psalms about David. He is preoccupied with the forever clause that is never far from his thoughts, writing and life. He not only wishes to dwell in the house of the Lord forever but he wants the Lord to dwell in him and his household forever. No matter how poor his parenting skills were, David wishes to believe that his household will reign forever. He actually hedges on that slightly more in the Psalms than he does in the other scriptures, but that forever clause is a perpetual preoccupation.

This little introduction is by no means meant to sour you on David or your favorite psalm whether the 23rd Psalm or otherwise. Rather it is to illustrate as we have in our other works, especially on the Original Testament, that beauty and eternal truths can be gleaned here and there despite the heavy contaminated background. The wheat and chaff must coexist for the time being in order for the wheat to reach maturity at harvest as suggested by no less than Jesus in the New Testament.

Steve

PSALMS 1- 150

26.   Psalm Twenty-six (05/01/23)
27.   Psalm Twenty-seven (05/11/23)
28.   Psalm Twenty-eight (05/11/23)
29.   Psalm Twenty-nine (05/11/23)
30.   Psalm Thirty (05/11/23)
31.   Psalm Thirty-one (05/11/23)
32.   Psalm Thirty-two (05/11/23)
33.   Psalm Thirty-three (05/11/23)
34.   Psalm Thirty-four (05/11/23)
35.   Psalm Thirty-five (05/12/23)
36.   Psalm Thirty-six (05/12/23)
37.   Psalm Thirty-seven (05/12/23)
38.   Psalm Thirty-eight (05/22/23)
39.   Psalm Third6-nine (05/19/23)
40.   Psalm Forty (05/19/23)
41.   Psalm Forty-one (05/21/23)
42.   Psalm Forty-two (05/21/23)
43.   Psalm Forty-three (05/21/23)
44.   Psalm Forty-four (05/22/23)
45.   Psalm Forty-five (05/22/23)
46.   Psalm Forth-six (05/22/23)
47.   Psalm Forty-seven (05/22/23)
48.   Psalm Forty-eight (05/22/23)
49.   Psalm Forty-nine (05/22/23)
50.   Psalm Fifty (05/22/23)
51.   Psalm Fifty-one (05/22/23)
Psalm-Fifty-one (#2) (06/06)
52.   Psalm Fifty-two (05/22/23)
53.   Psalm Fifty-three
54.   Psalm Fifty-four
55.   Psalm Fifty-five
56.   Psalm Fifty-six
57.   Psalm Fifty-seven
58.   Psalm Fifty-eight
59.   Psalm Fifty-nine (06/13/23)

60. Psalm Sixty (06/13/23)
61. Psalm Sixty-one (06/13/23)
62. Psalm Sixty-two (06/13/23)
63. Psalm Sixty-three (06/15/23)
64. Psalm Sixty-four (06/15/23)
65. Psalm Sixty-five (06/15/23)
66. Psalm Sixty-six (06/15/23)
67. Psalm Sixty-seven (06/16/23)
68. Psalm Sixty-eight (06/16/23)
69. Psalm Sixty-nine (06/16/23)
70. Psalm Seventy (06/17/23)
71. Psalm Seventy-one (06/17/23)
72. Psalm Seventy-two (06/17/23)
73. Psalm Seventy-three (06/17/23)
74. Psalm Seventy-four (06/17/23)
75. Psalm Seventy-five (06/19/23)
76. Psalm Seventy-six (06/19/23)
77. Psalm Seventy-seven (06/19/23)
78. Psalm Seventy-eight (06/22/23)
79. Psalm Seventy-nine (06/22/23)
80. Psalm Eighty (06/22/23)
81. Psalm Eighty-one (06/22/23)
82. Psalm Eighty-two (06/24/23)
83. Psalm Eighty-three (06/24/23)
84. Psalm Eight-four (06/24/23)
85. Psalm Eight-five (06/24/23)
86. Psalm Eighty-six (06/24/23)
87. Psalm Eighty-seven (06/24/23)
88. Psalm Eighty-eight (06/24/23)
89. Psalm Eighty-nine (06/24/23)
90. Psalm Ninety (06/24/23)
91. Psalm Ninety-one (06/24/23)
92. Psalm Ninety-two (06/24/23)
93. Psalm Ninety-three (06/24/23)
94. Psalm Ninety-four (06/24/23)

95. Psalm Ninety-five (07/22/23)
96. Psalm Ninety-six (07/22/23)
97. Psalm Ninety-seven (07/22/23)
98. Psalm Ninety-eight (07/22/23)
99. Psalm Ninety-nine (06/28/23)
100. Psalm One Hundred (06/28/23)
101. Psalm One Hundred One (06/28/23)
102. Psalm One Hundred Two (06/28/23)
103. Psalm One Hundred Three (06/28/23)
104. Psalm One Hundred Four (06/28/23)
105. Psalm One Hundred Five (06/28/23)
106. Psalm One Hundred Six (06/28/23)
107. Psalm One Hundred Seven (06/28/23)
108. Psalm One Hundred Eight (06/28/23)
109. Psalm One Hundred Nine (06/28/23)
110. Psalm One Hundred Ten (06/28/23)
111. Psalm One Hundred Eleven (06/28/23)
112. Psalm One Hundred Twelve (06/28/23)
113. Psalm One Hundred Thirteen (06/28/23)
114. Psalm One Hundred Fourteen (06/28/23)
115. Psalm One Hundred Fifteen (06/28/23)
116. Psalm One Hundred Sixteen (06/28/23)
117. Psalm One Hundred Seventeen (06/28/23)
118. Psalm One Hundred Eighteen (06/28/23)
119. Psalm One Hundred Nineteen (06/28/23)
120. Psalm One Hundred Twenty (06/28/23)
121. Psalm One Hundred Twenty-one (06/28/23)
122. Psalm One Hundred Twenty-two (06/28/23)
123. Psalm One Hundred Twenty-three (06/28/23)
124. Psalm One Hundred Twenty-four (06/28/23)
125. Psalm One Hundred Twenty-five (06/28/23)
126. Psalm One Hundred Twenty-six (06/28/23)
127. Psalm One Hundred Twenty-seven (06/30/23)
128. Psalm One Hundred Twenty-eight (06/30/23)
129. Psalm One Hundred Twenty-nine (06/30/23)

130. Psalm One Hundred Thirty (06/30/23)
131. Psalm One Hundred Thirty-one (06/30/23)
132. Psalm One Hundred Thirty-two (06/30/23)
133. Psalm One Hundred Thirty-three (07/02/23)
134. Psalm One Hundred Thirty-four (07/02/23)
135. Psalm One Hundred Thirty-five (07/02/23)
136. Psalm One Hundred Thirty-six (07/02/23)
137. Psalm One Hundred Thirty-seven (07/02/23)
138. Psalm One Hundred Thirty-eight (07/02/23)
139. Psalm One Hundred Thirty-nine (07/02/23)
140. Psalm One Hundred Forty (07/02/23)
141. Psalm One Hundred Forty-one (07/02/23)
142. Psalm One Hundred Forty-two (07/02/23)
143. Psalm One Hundred Forty-three (07/02/23)
144. Psalm One Hundred Forty-four (07/02/23)
145. Psalm One Hundred Forty-five (07/02/23)
146. Psalm One Hundred Forty-six (07/02/23)
147. Psalm One Hundred Forty-seven (07/02/23)
148. Psalm One Hundred Forty-eight (07/02/23)
149. Psalm One Hundred Forty-nine (07/02/23)
150. Psalm One Hundred Fifty (0702/23)
151. Psalm One Hundred Nineteen

Psalm 1

Regardless of whether or not we feel David wrote a particular Psalm his name is so attached to the book that we tend to get in that mood of thinking whenever we read any particular psalm, even if scholars are pretty certain that he did not write it. With the first Psalm, we are naturally placed in that position because there are the type of blessings that David so often refers to, and for which he has been known. We feel the blessings of the 23rd Psalm and the echoes of the still waters reverberate in the first Psalm.

The opening sentence is a classic example where one is called Blessed when they do not walk in step with the wicked or stand with sinners. The poetry of Eugene Peterson in the message is well put when he says how well God must like you. Most versions of this first sentence retain the poetry that involves walking and standing and sitting, as if to note that one may find themselves in the domain of the wicked, no matter what action or lack of action that they are engaged in.

In contrast to this is the righteous individual who obtains delight in the law of the Lord. Indeed, the implication is at least that these sinners have perceived delight in their actions, and wish to engage us in a shared delight, or perhaps a shared demise in which delight was the pretension. Meanwhile, because the wicked can present to us whether we are walking or standing or sitting, it becomes imperative that the righteous make efforts to meditate day and night.

Accordingly, we could add to the walking, standing, sitting the concept of sleeping or lying down, in the ways the wicked are trying to ensnare the righteous. We then move onto the beautiful symbolism of nature with the tree planted by streams of water, producing fruit at the proper time without withering any of its leaves. As a reward for this type of behavior, we are told that such a person prospers in whatever they do. We do not feel that such statement is an effort to extol the prosperity gospel.

This challenge to the prosperity gospel seems to revert in the next section when we are told that the the antithesis of the righteous being blessed for their righteousness is the wicked being punished for their wickedness. Yet a close examination notes that the wicked are being punished by nature in reaping what they sow. They are blown away by nature. Because they are not resolute, they cannot themselves stand in judgment. They cannot sit with the righteous.

If we complete the earlier triad of walking sitting and standing, then the wicked cannot walk humbly with their God either. This appears not as a judgement or punishment by God, but rather a natural consequence of a sinful life rather than a meditative life. The righteous meditate day and night. This is not the extreme of the monk in the monastery or Zen students but rather those who delight in the simple laws of God along with constant introspection. They don't mock others because they know at some level that they are the same as the person being mocked. A constant focus on meditation does not allow time for other such activities.

Psalm 2

When we cleanse Psalm number two from the anthropo-morphism and the temptation to read into prophecy some-thing that was never intended, what are we left over with? Let us take a look at the anthropomorphism first, and then examine what else we may. When we look at the anthro-pomorphism, we see a god that is either angry or laughing and not a whole lot left over. The song begins with a rhe-torical question of why people would conspire against God even when they get together.

Apparently, God finds this funny and laughs in what appears to be a derisive laugh by scoffing along with this. Next comes a rebuke with anger. Ultimately the kings of the Earth are given a recommendation to serve God with fear and trembling. The only apparent way that they can get away from the anger of God is to kiss his son, because after all the temperament of God and the wrath can flare up in a moment.

The point from start to finish with this song is that God simply cannot be beaten. You need to get on his side, including that of his adopted son. We need to be careful about the concept of presentism or interpreting this as a reference to the future, as in the son of God. In fact, the reference to the son of God is the author, and not a future Messiah. Going forward with this proposition you will see you later on that people are to kiss the author or God will be angry.

On the surface, we have this seemingly placid Psalm with bookends that begin with a rhetorical question of how could one conspire against God and ends with a blessing for all who take refuge in him. In between we have numerous warnings and a God who is mostly destructive and full of anger and vengeance and wrath at the moment of a drop of a hat. We have a seemingly narcissistic individual who somehow believes that he has earned the blessing of God to be called his son, and be kissed in order to appease an angry god.

The interesting thing here is that the narcissistic author has done nothing that we are told of any way to secure the favor of this vengeful and angry God. They are we to believe that God chooses to favor someone just for the sport of it and accordingly to display anger towards someone just for the sport of it? Perhaps we get some clue in the admonition of the author, that tells the kings, to be wise, and the rulers of the Earth, to serve the Lord with fear and trembling.

We would do well to be cautious when we look at versus six and seven. Here we have the concept of a king installed on a holy mountain. This is followed by the statement that you are my son and today I have become your father. This sounds so much like the statement that God makes after the baptism of Jesus so much so that we are tempted to invoke this as a prophecy of that which is to come. Let us suggest that we cannot change narcissistic thinking in others, but we can at least ourselves move beyond anthropomorphism.

Psalm 3

Before the beginning of Psalm number three we have the revelation that this is a psalm of David when he fled from his son Absalom. We may recall that Absalom had risen in revolt. Ultimately Absalom dies in this insurrection. Nonetheless, we must keep in mind that David professes to love him deeply. In fact, David may respect Absalom at some level for doing what Absalom did when he defended the honor of his sister from one of his half-brothers incestual rape.

When we read Psalm number three, we do not sense that connection of love with the son from whom he is alienated. Rather this is one of the woe is me psalms by David. Indeed, David laments how many enemies he has and that he is being derided by people who presumably are not his enemies, but have been his former allies. He puts the assertion out there that the naysayers are noting that God will not deliver him.

David counters this with the notion that God has put a shield around him. Accordingly, David is able to lift his head high. David claims that he is getting answers from God from the holy mountain. Accordingly, David is able to lay down and sleep in peace, knowing that he will be sustained, even though his enemies, assail him on every side. Although David may be sleeping soundly, despite the impending potential harm all around, it is God that David wishes to awaken.

After this little self-talk by David, he feels empowered to tell God to arise as though God may have been slumbering, and not acting on behalf of his servant David. David then proceeds to tell God what to do, which includes striking all of his enemies in the face to break their jaw and their teeth. This would include, of course, the very son Absalom, who meets a death that was arguably set in motion by the type of thinking in this Psalm.

This self talk by David has emboldened him with confidence to tell the Lord what to do. Perhaps his general who ultimately kills Absalom, heard this very Psalm before killing the insurrectionist Absalom. Of course, David wishes to challenge the pride of God, by noting that deliverance comes ultimately from the Lord. David concludes this psalm by wishing for blessings on the people of God.

This blessing, of course, is understood to be the people in the camp of David and not necessarily anyone else. When we read this Psalm we would do well too examine it from the emotions of David and the historical setting more so than a divine inspiration. Indeed, when we acknowledge only the notion that this is merely divinely inspired, and not a fearful David, running from his life and trying to recall his former glory, then we to run the risk in our present time of noting that God is on our side because we follow the only truth that God knows.

David was right in a sense in that somebody needed to wake up. That may not have been God. In addition, David may well have been wrong to presume that he should himself be sleeping and resting calmly when there is both family turmoil, and national turmoil that he may have contributed to and perhaps could have been solved-if he himself wakes up to reality.

Psalm 4

With psalm number four we once again see the mighty David telling God what to do. Basically, David says you better answer me when I am calling to you God. Then there is a little bit of flattery to clarify that it is my righteous God as if David not only owns God, but owns the adjectives to describe God as though God needed some adjectives. David, indeed, appears fairly bold given that apparently, he is in distress and needs mercy.

All of this occurs in the first verse. We are then, almost led to believe that this is going to be a dialogue back-and-forth between God and David. Verse two sounds very much like something God could say. How long will you people turn my glory into shame and love, delusions, and seek false gods? The only problem though is that it is still David talking, and we then come to realize that this man of pride is talking about his own glory being turned into shame.

David wishes to drive the point home that God has set them apart because he is faithful and that God will hear him when he calls to him. Once again, when we come to verse 4 it is almost as though God could be seen what is spoken in terms of trembling, but not sinning and search your heart and be silent. Next David is giving the command to appease God by offering sacrifice and trusting in the Lord.

If the front door flattery by David to God does not bring the desired results David is willing at the end of this Psalm to go to the back door. If after all, he asked God if you don't bring us prosperity who will? How can even God object to a command from his anointed king David, to fill his heart with joy, while the grain and wine abounds. Yes, David presumed that he will lay down in peace and sleep only because God alone allows him to dwell in safety.

Psalm 5

With the summary, let us proceed top to bottom with this Psalm. David begins by telling the Lord to listen to him and to consider him and then once again to hear his cry for help. David knows that his plea for help is also a prayer. He becomes sycophantic when he says that the Lord hears his voice in the morning. After that request, David waits expectantly. After all, God is summoned, who is not pleased with wickedness or arrogance.

Interestingly, nowhere in this Psalm does David make his case for not being arrogant or being wicked. Rather is seems presumed that David is not among those who do wrong, and nor is he bloodthirsty or deceitful because God would detest such an individual. Apparently, we are to believe that someone who attempts to tell God several times what to do is not arrogant. However, it gets more dramatic after that. In verse seven will you see that David is able to come into the Lord's house by virtue of God's great love. This is interesting that David says next, he can bow down with reverence toward the holy temple, because David himself was not able to build the house of God because he was a man of war.

After being a bit sycophantic, it is time for David to tell God once again what to do in verse eight. In verse eight, David proceeds to tell God to lead him in his righteousness because of the enemies of David. It is not clear why God should automatically lead David because of David's enemies but somehow David makes us believe that such is automatic. With that he commands God to make his way straight before David. He points out that his enemies cannot be trusted with a single word, and that they are full of malice.

Next David utters a delightfully wicked phrase that his enemies collective throat is an open grave. In verse number 10 David, once again tells God what to do by declaring his enemy is guilty. He tells God to let their intrigues be their downfall. It is not clear why he would ask for the intrigues of his enemies to be their downfall because this seems to imply that they themselves could not intrigue God to lead them. Rather, David tells God to banish them for their many sins because of rebellion.

In classic fashion, David turns immediately from this ill wishing to his enemies to asking a blessing for all who take refuge in God. The protection is requested as well. All somebody has to do is love the name of God to be able to rejoice. After all, surely God will bless the righteous This challenge to God to surely bless the righteous is reminiscent of Abraham, challenging God that surely, he would not destroy the righteous with the wicked. We might recall that the indirect answer to that question by Abraham to God was indeed, that God would destroy the wicked with the righteous. Nonetheless we still imagine that like David, we can distinguish ourselves from the wicked.

Psalm 6

Psalm number six is another woe is me Psalm by David. David begins this Psalm by telling God once again what to do and what not to do. Specifically, he tells God not to rebuke David in his anger or discipline David in his wrath. David asks for mercy because he is faint. He wants healing because his bones are in agony, and his soul is in deep anguish. Like most of us, David wants to know how long this will go on.

It is interesting to note that David request mercy and relief from the anger and wrath, and feeling faint, but does not acknowledge any wrongdoing to have received this sensation. If one of the meanings of repent is to turn than effectively, David is asking God to repent in verse four and deliver David. He does become sycophantic and say that God to do this because of God's unfailing love. He continues his sycophantic moan by noting that no one can proclaim God's name, or praise him from the grave.

Yes, this is moaning and groaning as David himself uses the term in verse six. He is in fact, weeping so many tears that he does it day and night, and drenches his couch because of this. This causes his eyes to be weak from the sorrow. Then, for the first time in this song, David blames his foes for his woes. He then asks for distance from those who are evil because God has heard his weeping. David then becomes once again presumptuous that God has heard his cry from mercy and accepted his prayer. Surely this will overwhelm and shame his enemies, in a rather sudden fashion.

Psalm 7

Psalm number seven is another woe is me Psalm by David, which is framed by giving credit to God at the start and thanks at the end of the psalm. The problem is that David cannot even get through the first verse without turning the emphasis to himself. He feels the urge to have God save and deliver him from all who pursue him. After all they will rip him to pieces with no one there to rescue him.

Then we have the peculiar reference to an apparent accusation, which is never spelled out when David is turning back to God, in verse three and placing a curse on himself. He says if I have done this.... However, we are never told what this is. Nonetheless, David knows that if he has done this and there's guilt on his hands and there is any suggestion that he has treated his ally inappropriately, or even robbed his foe, then he wishes his own enemies to pursue him, and overtake him, and trample him to the ground.

David is fairly confident though that he has not made these compromises because in verse six he again tells God what to do. It is time for God to arise in his anger against the rage of his enemies. God needs to wake up and do justice. Then the common people can gather around God and his throne. God will also serve as judge to the people, but more importantly, for David, God will vindicate David. Indeed, God will vindicate David according to David's own righteousness, as opposed to the righteousness of God. Of course we have to throw in the integrity thing for David as well.

David will next turn and acknowledge the righteousness of God provided God do his job and make the righteous secure and deal with the violence of the wicked. David once again turns to the duties of God as a righteous judge to display his wrath particularly against those who are evil. Indeed, the evil and wicked will suffer from God exploring their conscience with their own violence coming back up on their heads. After this destruction, David has to wrap this up with giving thanks to the lord because of his righteousness, and to sing God's praises.

Psalm 8

David must have been in a good mood when he wrote psalm number eight. This Psalm is all about praise and majesty for God. If we look at the framework of the beginning and the end of the psalm, we might think that it is another set up for the woe is me process that David is so noted for. However, that downside never occurs in this particular Psalm. It does have the symmetric quality of praise with majesty at the start, and the end with exactly the same wording at the conclusion.

In this Psalm, we do not have any distinct reference to the enemies of David. Rather there are enemies to be sure, but they are the enemies of God. This may be a veiled reference because preceding that is the notion that the praises of children and infants would overcome the enemies of God, and silence the foe and avenger. When one knows about David, it is difficult to not feel that this is about his enemies who are subdued, but have, of course become God's enemies.

David is enamored with the nature that God has created with the moon and the stars and the heavens, each in their own rightful place. Why would such a powerful and creative God care for a human beings. We do not get the answer to that question, but rather the awareness that God has made those human beings to be the rulers over God 's creation, and only slightly lower than that of the angels. Ah yes, when things are going well for David, like the rest of us, symmetry with internal beauty and eternal praise is flowing.

Psalm 9

Psalm number nine has an interesting introduction in the title. Like many of the Psalms, this is noted to be for the Director of music. We are told that it has a particular tune, which is the death of the son. It is not clear if this is in reference to David 's own son Absalom, who was an insurrectionist killed by one of David's generals. The translator of the title has capitalized the word Son perhaps to capture the Jesus and David linage connection, with Jesus as the figurative son of David.

This psalm is another victory psalm over the enemies of David. David is giving thanks and telling of the wonderful deeds of God and singing the praises of the highest because the enemies of David have turned back and stumble before God. David has his rights and a reasonable cause, as determined by the righteous judge that we know as God. Indeed, it is God who reviews the nations and destroys the wicked and even blots out their name.

The enemies of David will suffer endless ruin. Furthermore, even their memories will perish. Keep in mind that this is indeed exactly what happened to Uriah a devoted General who had a beautiful wife named Bathsheba. After David has his dalliance with her, he has Uriah put to death in an ignominious way. If this is what David does to his loyal generals, then certainly you do not want to be an enemy.

Psalm 10

Psalm number 10 is a taunting and berating Psalm. David initiates the psalm with asking God why he stands so far off and hides in times of trouble. Meanwhile, the wicked or arrogant are boasting about their cravings. Evil people apparently stick together because the wicked man blesses the greedy and reviles the Lord. Indeed, and his pride of the wicked man will not seek God, because there is no room for God.

Because nothing has ever shaken the wicked individual, they make an assumption that nothing of harm will ever come to them. They tell lies and give threats. The lye in ambush for the innocent, and the helpless. Then after all of his destruction, the wicked say that God will never notice because he covers his face and never sees. Are you listening God? David says it is time to wake up.

Surely God sees the evil that the wicked do. God sees the grief of the afflicted. David continues with the notion that victims commit themselves to God because God is the helper of those who are fatherless. The wicked will have a day of accountability. Interestingly, this is one of the few times that David seems to be challenging God to do some good for people, other than himself. David closes this song by recognizing the eternal nature of God as king and answering the oppression.

Psalm 11

Psalm number 11 is potentially a continuation of Psalm number 10. Of course, there are overlapping themes in the psalms that are recurrent as well. David begins the psalm by noting that he takes refuge in the Lord. He has apparently been given counsel to flee from his enemies, but he asks how he can do that even though the wicked have set their arrows against him and other people who are upright.

After all, what can the righteous do when their foundations are being destroyed. David knows though, that the Lord is in his holy temple and heavenly throne, while observing that destruction on earth, including the violence, and the wicked that he hates with a passion. They will have their reward. The Lord is after all at the conclusion noted to be righteous and Justice loving. The upright will see his face. These statements foreshadow, the beatitudes in the sermon on the mount.

Psalm 12

Psalm number 12 seems to have the overtones of the woe is me David. However, the opening is more about woe is society. He sounds typical of the older, conservative generation who laments that the young people just don't have any faith or values for that matter. In his opening sentence he says that no one is faithful anymore, and that those who are loyal and vanished from the human race. He says everyone is a liar and a flatterer with deception in their hearts.

Naturally, David calls on God to silence all such individuals. We can almost read into this that somebody had obtained at least a minor victory over David and was bragging about that. David knows that such people even taunted God during their behavior. Now it is time for David to put words into God's mouth. He says that because the poor are plundered and the needy groan that God will arise and protect such. After all, the words of the Lord are flawless. When, taken at its face value, this Psalm suggest that God will protect the needy from the wicked, even if the needy people are not faithful.

Psalm 13

In Psalm 13 we see David returning to the woe is me, David. The question is how long God will forget him and hide his face from him. Just as Jacob had to wrestle with God years earlier now David must wrestle with his own thoughts. Day after day, he is filled with sorrow in his heart. David demands that God look on him and answer him and give light to his eyes unless he dies. To do so would cause his enemies to gloat. David suggests this is not a good thing, because David is the one who trusts in God's unfailing love. So, we have the David in the first verse saying that God has forgotten him and in the final verse that God has been good to him. Dare we ask if it is good to be forgotten by God? Is this not the question that Jesus asked in the New Testament? My God my God why have you forsaken me?

Psalm 14

David begins this Psalm by noting that the morally deficient say in their heart that there is no God. This implies that such may not be spoken of, or at even some level aware of fully mentally and yet the heart is saying very clearly that there is no God. they are without values, and therefore their actions are vile. Next, we have some of the extremes of David's utterances. He knows that there is no one who does good. Somehow though David knows that God looks down from heaven to see if you can find that one individual who is actually good.

It turns out that there is no such individual, but all of turned away and become corrupt. For emphasis David notes, there is no one who does good not even one. Such people David says nothing. David knows that they did devour his own people as though they were eating bread, but do not turn to God. David knows that the reward is not bread but dread, somehow though the righteous people are still present, despite what David said earlier. Though evildoers may exploit the poor, God is still their refuge. God will restore his people.

Psalm 15

Psalm number 15 is a question-and-answer Psalm. Whereas many of David's opening questions are about why God is hiding from him, this one begins with a question of who can dwell in God's sacred tent, and live on his holy mountain. The rest of the psalm explores who that might be. Specifically, it is the individual who is blameless and righteous and speaks the truth from the heart. There is no ill will or slander. He is a good neighbor. Furthermore, such an individual despises evil people, but honors those for fear of the Lord. They keep their oaths even when it is painful. They are unwavering in their mind. They are generous with money for the poor. Such individuals cannot be shaken. This is a foreshadowing of the beatitudes in the sermon on the mount.

Psalm 16

This psalm is a refuge song with David appealing to God for safety and security. He knows that apart from God that he can have no good thing. He will not be like other people who run after other gods. Rather, his security and inheritance are in praising God, who gives him counsel. This answer comes even at night through his heart. Above and beyond his heart, though his body will also rest secure because he will not be abandoned or allowed to decay.

Psalm 17

Psalm number 17 is a vindication psalm. David makes an appeal to the sensory side of God. He tells God in the first person to listen to his cry because his plea is just. Also, to hear his prayer because David is not deceitful. Furthermore, David wants to let God know that God sees what is right. Good for God. And maybe David. No, sir. David is a good guy. And you can probe his heart even at night time because he has no plans for evil and his mouth does not utter transgressions.

Furthermore, David is able to resist bribes. He follows God's commands and holds to the path of God without stumbling. The metaphors are rich when he says to God to keep David in the apple of his eye, and to hide David in the shadow of your wings. David desires protection from the wicked, who were to destroy him and have already surrounded him. Once again, David will tell God what to do by bringing such people down. In the meantime, David will be vindicated, and will see the face of God and will be satisfied with seeing his likeness.

Psalm 18

Psalm number 18 is much longer then many earlier Psalms and is a recognition by David from the deliverance from his enemies. He describes many phenomena of nature, and how God used such to deliver him. Of course, God did this ultimately because of the righteousness of David according to the Psalm, and according to the cleanliness of his hands, he was rewarded as we read in verse 20. After all, God did all of this rescue therapy because he delighted in David we are told. We were told by David himself that he is blameless from sin.

Psalm 19

Psalm number 19 is one of the purest psalms by David. Arguably, it is one of the most uncontaminated psalms by David in the sense that it is not full of vitriolic revenge against his enemies, or any self-gloating, or egotistical statements that surface episodically in other psalms. We shall make a brief comparison even to the 23rd Psalm, which is often considered the finest by David that he has to offer. As idyllic as this is, the 23rd Psalm may does not appear to match the purity of Psalm number 19.

David begins this psalm by declaring the glory of God as proclaimed by the heavens. The heavens speak day and night and reveal knowledge without speech, and without using words. Although there is no sound, their voice goes out into all of the earth, including the ends of the world, this is rich metaphor, arguably more so even then the 23rd Psalm. He likens the sun as being stored in a tent that God has pitched. When it comes out of the tent, it is like a bride groom coming out from his chamber. It is like a champion who is rejoicing to run his course.

This sun metaphor makes his circuit and deprives nothing of its warmth. This is the prelude for recognizing the perfect law of the Lord, which is refreshing for the soul. The precepts of the Lord give joy to the heart, and the commands of the Lord are radiant, just like the sun referenced earlier. This gives light to the eyes. The fear of the Lord is eternal and is pure. Of course, all of the decrees of the Lord, are not only firm, but righteous and more precious than gold and sweeter than honey.

Keeping these precepts carries with it a great reward. But here David shows a rare moment in the sense that he is introspective and raises that introspective question of who can discern their own mistakes. David prays the deepest prayer when he asked to be forgiven for his hidden faults. He asked to be kept from his willful sins, so that they really may not rule over him. In this psalm he does not take it for granted that his words would be automatically pleasing to God or his meditations, but he does ask for that grace.

When we contrast psalm number 19 with psalm number 23 it may be helpful to remove our preconceptions of our beloved psalm. However, as rich as the imagery is, it does reflect some anthropomorphic measures and words such as God, like David, is a shepherd who provides for everything, including rest and refreshment for his soul. He is a guide for David through the darkest moments, leading him to abandon fear. The shepherd's staff and his rod are comforting tools for David.

Yes, as poetic as this is, David cannot resist the notion that God is going to do something special for him like prepare his own table. More so, this must be done in the presence of his enemies. Most of us cannot think of much less than gloating about such opportunity. Naturally such an individual would feel anointed, and the goodness and fortune would follow them all of their days. Of course, David would be blessed to be dwelling in the house of the Lord forever.

Psalm 20

David expresses his benevolence to other people in distress in the opening part of this Psalm. Perhaps because he himself has suffered so much distress is he able to relate to others in similar predicament. It almost sounds like an Irish blessing that he is giving individuals in distress far more than it is a prayer to the Lord God. May God remember all your sacrifices, and accept your burnt offerings, he says. May he give you the desires of your heart and make all your plans succeed. He repeats this theme several times. He feels that doing so will lead to victory and joy.

We see the transition moment of this psalm occur in verse six in which David says that he knows God gives victory to his anointed. This, of course would be David. It is also a distinction of absolute knowledge that he is professing compared to the earlier request wishes, and Irish blessing process. David distinguishes those who trust in chariots and horses, as opposed to people, like himself who trust in the name of the Lord God. It is time for God to give victory to the king, and answer those who call upon him.

Psalm 21

Psalm number 21 is an effusive Psalm in which David showers God with praise because God has seen the benefit of blessing David. He has given David many victories and granted him his heart's desire and not withholding anything that David has requested. David has been granted a crown of pure gold. He was given the life he asked for by God. In fact, it is an eternal life that he was granted. No doubt God did this, because David trusts in the Lord.

Of course, such a God has other duties to do just like an earthly king wood. God has to get a hold of his enemies and his foes and burn them in a blazing furnace. After they have been swallowed up in the wrath of God, the fire will then consume them just to make sure that the job gets done. But alas, that is not enough as their descendants will be destroyed from the earth as well of course. If after all of this is said and done, David will sing the Lord's praises.

Psalm 22

Because the Bible is full of phrases and prophecies showing how Jesus is from the house of David, we tend to read into things that are attributed to David as prophesying something for Jesus. Psalm number 22 is a classic example which opens up with my god my god why have you forsaken me. In fact, David beseeches God Day and night to no avail. This is reminiscent of Jesus, who utters the same phrases on the cross.

Next David employs for God to answer his prayer because his ancestors put their trust in him. This is his plea, even though he says that he himself is only a worm and not a man who is mocked by everyone. If God is listening, he realizes that David is being put down because he trusts in God and it is the duty of God to rescue him from such taunting. After all, God brought David out of the womb and made him trust God. David tells God that you're far from him because of nearby trouble, and with no one else to help.

David feels surrounded by forces of evil that he cannot overcome. Again, we see the reference of piercing his hands and his feet much like Jesus on the cross. Also, all of his bones are on display and people stare and gloat over him and divide his clothes among them. This is a strong foreshadowing of what happened to Jesus on the cross. Still David appeals to God to deliver him under such circumstances.

After this self-talk, David has gathered momentum and stars to point out how God has not despised or scorned the suffering of those who are afflicted. He has not hidden his face from those who cry for help. No, indeed the poor will be satisfied. Those who seek the Lord will praise him. This will be extended to the ends of the Earth with all nations. Posterity will also serve God. The forever clause of David's family on the throne remains his perpetual concern.

Psalm 23

Psalm number 23 is considered the masterpiece by David. It is the idyllic setting in nature in which David's own occupation is presupposed by no less than God. Once again we have the foreshadowing of Jesus Christ who is also the Great Shepherd. With such as his shepherd, David lacks nothing. He is tranquil and at peace with a serenity that guides him to those tranquil waters.

Indeed, God, as the good shepherd guards David through the darkest of times, and the most fearful places in his life. What is there to fear? David is comforted by the very rod and staff of the good shepherd. David will have his head anointed with oil. His cup will overflow. Goodness, love and mercy will follow him all of his life as he dwells in God's house forever.

All is well and good if we leave it at that. But David is not the type to leave things alone. We have seen how he will exact his vengeance on several people on his deathbed that he has seemingly forgiven many years earlier. So too is the one dark side of this otherwise wonderful psalm. David has to have his blessings enjoyed in the presence of his enemies who can only look on and be envious. With this one verse we see the true colors of David potentially staining this otherwise beautiful poem.

With one stone David can kill the giant. With one stone David can kill wild animals. With one indiscretion with Bathsheba he can alter his own legacy and cast a shadow upon it. With one word he can have his top general Uriah set up for death merely because he had the audacity to be partnered and faithful to Bathsheba before David. With one word he can have people executed who saved his life such as Joab. With one word he can have one of his wives who saved his life Micah, exiled and suffer the loss of children. With one verse David shows that even divinely inspired individuals have a very human side.

Psalm 24

If the order of the psalms reflects a timeline of continuity, then Psalm number 24 is a wonderful extension of psalm number 23. Arguably it has more purity in the sense that there are no dark sides or signs of retribution or gloating in the presence of enemies. We have rather a humble David, who is in recognition of the majesty of God, with the dominion over all of the world that was created by God.

It is naturally desirable to be able to communicate with such a God. Realistically, who can do so? David supplies that answer by noting that the person who has clean hands and a pure heart, and who does not trust in idols, or swear by a false God. What we find most interesting through the development of the rest of the Psalm is that David does not claim to be such an individual. We will not belabor that point here but we do refer the interested reader to our book on David and Michelangelo, where these themes are, indeed, exposed more at length.

As much as David is gifted at using the metaphors of nature, he finds a new measure of expression in this Psalm. In this setting, we see David employing the concept of physical structures, such as gates and doors, having heads that they will lift up to praise the king of glory, who is to be quite clear, the Lord God, and not David. In fact, twice he employs this metaphor image. To make sure that everyone understands that the king of glory is the Lord God, and not David, David spells this out in the last verse.

Psalm 25

Psalm number 25 is another do not let me down God I'm counting on you Psalm. David opens with the statement that he trusts in God so don't let me be put to shame. Don't let my enemy's triumph over me. After all, anyone who hopes in God will never be put to shame. But if you were talking about shame, it will come to those who are treacherous, despite not having any reason to be so.

David then realizes that, perhaps he better learn what the righteous path is from God, so that he will not stray. Maybe then he will get some great mercy and love from the source. He does recognize sins that he has committed, but those were in his youth, and he feels could be pardoned. The same with his rebellious nature. After all, God is a God of love. That God does indeed instruct sinners because it is what a good God does. Of course, it helps if an individual is humble.

David goes on to acknowledge that his iniquity is great in this particular Psalm. However, for his own name's sake, God is implored to forgive David. After all, the ways of God are loving and faithful. This, of course, will lead to prosperity for any who fear the Lord and follow his instructions. God even has confidence and confides in such people. God shares the covenant with such people.

David turns next to his series of requests to God that he be released from the snare that he is in. He is after all lonely and afflicted. He is troubled in his heart. He is distressed and knows there is an advantage to removing his sins. After all, his enemies are numerous. He appeals to God at the close of this song to rescue him again to save him from shame room for good measure David throws in delivering all of Israel, grabs just in case God would not do it for David 's sake alone.

Psalm 26

Psalm number 26 is another vindication Psalm. Indeed, vindicate is the first word of this Psalm. David feels that he has led a blameless life, having trusted God without faltering. He even implores God to put him to the test and examine both his heart and his mind, because he has always been mindful of the unfailing love of God. David then outlines a number of things that he does not associate with such as hypocrites and deceitful people, and evil doers, and the wicked in general.

No sir. David washes his hands in his innocence. David wishes to exalt God by going to his house, because he knows God dwells there. David does not wish to have his lot cast with the sinners. No to repeat, David feels that he has led a blameless life and deserves mercy and deliverance. He will stand on level ground in the great congregation and praise God.

Psalm 27

Psalm number 27 is a rallying cry. David appears to be in a position where he is once again being besieged by his enemies. He gives the impression of needing to muster his courage. Naturally he begins by appealing to God as his light and salvation. This is of course not the salvation that New Testament believers have come to believe in but rather a salvation from his enemies.

After acknowledging God as his stronghold, David asks the rhetorical question of whom should he be afraid. You might argue psychologically that he gives the answer immediately after that. The wicked who would devour him. Also his foes and enemies and armies who have besieged him. No, under these circumstances David will not even fear war. Under these most difficult times David is confident.

He hedges on his presumptions of the protection by God immediately after he has rallied his courage. He asks the one thing from God which is to dwell in the house of the Lord all of his days. He merely wants to gaze at the beauty of the Lord in his temple and meditate on that. David goes on to include no less than 5 places that one might find God.

In addition to the house and temple, we have the generic dwelling. Next we have shelter. Finally a reference is made to the most ancient form of abode for God which is the tent similar which is what the Israelites experienced in the wilderness long before David had the desire to build a temple for God. Some would even call to question whether this was actually written after David since there is some reference to the temple which he was forbidden to build because of his warring nature.

In this abode of God series, we encounter images that are present in the 23rd Psalm with the notion that David will dwell in the house of the Lord forever. Still David must supplicate God to be merciful. After all, David seeks the face of God. This is something that not even Moses standing on the mountaintop was able to do in the presence of God. Nor was Abraham able to see the face of God. Such history known to David does not thwart him.

By this time in the Psalm David has become emboldened. He can tell God what to do and what not to do. Do not hide your face from me. Do not reject me or forsake me like my own mother and father did. No God. Teach me and instruct me in that path that is righteous and mentioned also in Psalm 23. Do not turn me over to my oppressors, which by the way, is a sign that already David is being controlled by alien forces.

No, David will finish with confidence that he will see the goodness of God. Is this not the same as seeing the face of God. Is this not a manifest expression and prelude to the Matthew chapter 25 story of the sheep and goats. There both sides ask the basic question: when did we see the Lord. The answer is unambiguous. You saw God when you saw humans hungry, when you saw them lonely, when you saw them in prison, when you saw them naked. Only those who responded to those needs have a perpetual vision of God.

Finally either David or the person writing on his behalf or attempting to represent his style of thinking does come out with some phrasing at the end of the Psalm. As confident as David is in the goodness of the Lord (translation: God will protect me from the bad guys and subsequently bless him), he recognizes the key ingredient and mentions it twice. David needs to wait for the Lord. David cannot rush ahead of God and expect blessings. One cannot see anything when rushing without God.

Psalm 28

Psalm number 28 is a silence Psalm. By this we mean that David perceives God as being silent. More notably is that he perceives God as turning a deaf ear in th first verse. This is emphasized a second time in that first verse. With the second reference there is a conditional notion that if God remained silent, then David will be like those who go down to the pit which is the anachronistic phrase for hell.

Verse 2 begins with another plea to be heard. Hear my cry for Mercy as I call to you for help. After all, David is lifting his hands much like Moses raised his hands. Those hands point to the holy place. David does not deserve to be drug away with the wicked, he feels. So naturally he needs to remind God of this. Such people may talk cordially with their neighbors but harbor malice in their hearts. If that is not a formula for embedded illness then my 40 years as a physician have been misplaced.

After hurling a few Irish curses at such people, David will turn once again to God as his fortress. He will praise God because finally God is listening to him. David knows he needs Mercy which implies a deficit, a need, and a position of compromise. David will then praise God with a joyous heart. Then he will recognize that this is more than a God for his selfish purposes, but rather for all the people of the covenant. God is both their shepherd and salvation. This is indeed ongoing affirmation about David as prefiguring Christ.

Psalm 29

Psalm number 29 is a praise psalm from start to finish. There is no woe is me perspective. There is no save me from my enemies. There is only praise to God with glory. God is found in nature. Indeed, God's voice is experienced there with lightening, strong and wild animals, trees, etc. Finally, the last nature reference is to the flood. Now we don't know if this is reference to The Flood of Noah. If so it is about the power of God to both destroy and renew life. The psalm closes with recognition to the eternal nature of God along with the peaceful nature.

Psalm 30

Psalm 30 is another symmetrical psalm where Davis starts and ends with praise to God for rescuing David from the jaws of his enemies. David was mourning in sackcloth because of being in the clutches of his enemies. Yet David called to God and was rescued even from Hell or the pit.

Even so, David mentions God's anger as being short in duration.

David has made his praise. Yet he does not feel delivered. He recalls how God hid his face from him. David reminds God that there is nothing gained if David is silenced. God may have created mankind out of dust as we read in the Genesis but David feels obligated to remind God that dust cannot give praise. Still David recognizes that he needs Mercy. The formula here is basically give God some praise and demand some Mercy. Basically this is the formula for the Lord's Prayer.

Psalm 31

Psalm number 31 is a refuge Psalm. David claims to have taken refuge in God and therefore desires not to be put to shame, but to be delivered by the righteousness of God and into the righteousness of God. David request God to turn his ear to him And come to his rescue. Apparently taking refuge in God or saying, so it's not enough to actually feel rescued.

Once again, we see the hedge factor and sycophantic David pointing out to God that, since God is the rock and fortress for David, then for the sake of God's own name, to be lead and guided. Meanwhile, David's request for God to be kept free from the trap set for him, because after all once again, God is his refuge.

David somehow senses that such measure is not enough and so he distinguishes himself from those who follow worthless idols. David is different because he will be glad and rejoice in the love of God who saw the affliction of

David and the anguish of his soul and would not give him over to the enemy.

Despite all this, David still seems in distress as he himself notes, and he requests mercy from God, because of his weakness, and his sorrow and his grief in both body and soul. In fact, the entire life of David is consumed by anguish and groaning. Even his bones have grown weak. Indeed, because of David's enemies, he is the utter contempt of his neighbors, and the object of dread, even to his closest friends. David has been forgotten and he feels as though he were dead.

Now is the time for David to turn back to supplicating God and pleading his case for mercy. After all he trusts God and his times are in the hands of God. He asks for the face of God to shine upon his servant David. After all, God has unfailing love, and according to David, he should not be put to shame because he has cried out to God. On the other hand, those wicked people do need to be put to shame he says, as though once again, to distinguish himself from such people.

Finally, David closes this psalm in his usual symmetrical fashion by praising the Lord, who has heard his cry for mercy. He then versus a universal recognition for other righteous people.

Psalm 32

Psalm number 32 begins with blessings for those whose sins and transgressions are forgiven and covered. In fact, this is a theme that is repeated three times in the first two verses. David then turns to a perplexing paradox, where he states that when he kept silent, his bones wasted away.

However, they wasted away through his groaning all day long. It is difficult to conceive how he was both silent and groaning at the same time. However, it is clear that David blames God for having his heavy hand on him and sapping his strength like the heat of summer.

It was at that low point that David acknowledged his sin and iniquity, and made a confession of his transgressions. At that time, he was forgiven of the guilt of his sin. According all faithful people should pray to God, while God could still be found. One wonders if this is an implication that the anthropomorphic god goes into hiding, or if rather humans simply lose sight of how to find God. Speaking of hiding, though David calls God his hiding place along with his protection. Like many of the Psalms, this one has a symmetrical beginning with blessings, and ending with praise and rejoicing.

Psalm 33

Psalm number 33 is pretty much a praise song from start to finish. David sings the praises of the God who loves righteousness and justice. He sings the wonders of the creation of God. David distinguishes the temporal plans of nations and peoples from those of the eternal plans of God. Nonetheless the nation who serves God is also blessed. Nations are not delivered by their own strength or weapons, but deliverance comes from waiting in the hope for the Lord.

Psalm 34

This Psalm has an interesting heading in that we are told it is in regards to when David pretended to be insane in the presence of an enemy. This concept gives a new perspective to the 23rd song when David is to fear no evil in the valley of the shadow of death and recognizes that a table has been prepared for him in the presence of his enemies. Amazingly David is able to extol the Lord and praise him at all times in this insanity perspective. Somehow this gives hope for the afflicted.

Such people who are delivered from their fears, are radiant in their faces, and have no shame. In this psalm David claims to be poor, as though God did not attend to his prayers, and save him merely because of his status or wealth. Rather the angel of the Lord encamps around everyone who fears God, and will indeed deliver them. One only needs to use the sensory perceptions of taste and vision to see that God is good when an individual takes the refuge in God.

Next, it is time for David to give some lessons to the people whom he calls his children. Most notably is to fear the Lord. Also included is keeping the tongue from evil and the lips from telling lies. Seeking peace, and even pursuing it are paramount. God also has sensory perceptions with eyes that look on the righteousness and ears that are attentive to their cry. However, the anthropomorphic face of God is against those who do evil. Those ears of God hear the righteous people when they cry out and will be delivered from all of their troubles. the evil are not so fortunate as the servants of God who will be rescued.

Psalm 35

In Psalm 35 David will make his appeal to God right off the bat in order to contend against his enemies. David will anthropomorphize God by asking God to take up shield and armor. Actually, David tells God what to do. He tells God to say to David that God is the salvation of David.

Meanwhile an Irish blessing to disgrace those who seek the life of David. Of course, God must assist the process through his own angel.

After all, these adversaries of David got to him by sett a trap for him without any cause whatsoever. After they get their Karma, David can delight and rejoice. David is besieged by ruthless witnesses who questioned him on things that he knows nothing about. David claims to be repaid evil for the good he has done. This is despite the fact that when they were ill, he put on sackcloth and humbled himself with fasting. Nonetheless, his adversaries slandered him without ceasing, despite having no cause.

David accuses God has been an uninvolved onlooker. When this happens, David will give praise to God for deliverance from those who gloat over David and hate him without reason. Indeed, David, once again tells God what to do in the form of not being silent. After several Irish blessing on his enemies, David closes this Psalm by proclaiming the righteousness of God through praises all day long.

Psalm 36

David starts out Psalm 36 by noting he has a message from God in his heart concerning the wicked. This message is not earth shattering but is merely that there is no fear of God in the eyes of the wicked. Rather they flatter themselves and are full of deceit, and do not act wisely. This is in contrast to the love of God, which reaches to the heavens. The righteousness of this anthropomorphic God is like the highest mountains and the justice like the great deep. Meanwhile, God is someone that the righteous may take refuge in.

Psalm 37

Psalm number 37 is a psalm of contrasts between what happens to those who are evil, and what happens to those who trust in the Lord. Like many other Psalms, it has much from nature. There is the admonition to be patient and still before the Lord. David notes that God is laughing at the wicked, who have said measures to bring down the poor and downtrodden.

The second half of those Psalm focuses on the victory and blessings for those who are blameless and righteous. To be sure there is the usual contrast with the wicked. David, meanwhile, put in a plug for those who seek peace.

Psalm 38

Psalm 38 can perhaps be best appreciated by reading the first few verses in the translation by Eugene Peterson called the Message. In that version, we hear David telling God to take a deep breath and calm down and not be so hasty with his punishing rod. from there, David goes on to point out the extreme destruction to his body because of the wrath of God. Simultaneously David's guilt has overwhelmed him.

These measures are enough for friends and companions to avoid David. Even his neighbors stay far away. Nonetheless, David musters the courage to say that he will wait for God. indeed, David introduces that theme in about the middle of the psalm and carries it forward to the very end. This is a pattern a little bit different than the symmetrical Psalms.

Psalm 39 continues or 38 left off. David begins this by noting that he will watch his ways and his tone and even put a muzzle on his mouth. This included not even saying anything good. finally, David had enough of his signs and ask God to show him his lives, and the number of his days. However, David still maintains that his hope is in the Lord. however, despite that hope in the lord, David will blame God for his afflictions.

Psalm 39

Psalm number 39 is another Psalm and which David begins by telling God what to do and not to do. He tells God not to rebuke him with the God anger or to discipline him with the God wrath. Rather, he accuses God of having shot arrows that have pierced him. He accuses God of zapping his health in spring because of the wrath of God. It does take some ownership that he is suffering because of his sin. Then in verse 4 his knowledge is his guilt, which is overwhelming. He does take some ownership that he is suffering because of his sin. Then in verse four he knowledges is his guilt, which is overwhelmed him.

Meanwhile, the wounds of David are festering because of that sin and folly. Indeed the mighty David is humbled by these actions. Yet his health has been drained. He is left with groaning only and anguish in his heart. David has become like the legendary Job within that his friends and companions have avoided him because of his wounds. This makes it easy for those who wish to kill him to set their traps while scheming and lying.

David uses the sensory metaphors much like Job. He is like the deaf in the hearing impaired and the mute cannot speak. Then after his lamenting and about 2/3 of the way into the Psalm David notes that he will wait for God. David notes that he is about to fall and then his pain is always with him. David knows he needs to make a confession and mentions being troubled by his sin. However, people have become his enemies without any cause. The worst thing he feels is that he is being repaid evil when he has done good to other people. He closes the Psalm with his symmetrical play to not be forsaken.

Psalm 40

With this psalm, David is starting out in a bad place. He's in a slimy pit with mud and mire. Yet he claims that he is waited patiently for the Lord, and accordingly was delivered having his feet set on a firm place. He feels light on his feet and feels that he has been given a new song to praise God with. He knows that with this process many were experiencing fear of the Lord and put their trust in the Lord. Perhaps this is because of David's example.

Indeed, David knows, following this, that a person is blessed who puts his trust in the Lord and does not look to the proud or turn aside to the fake gods. He notes the many wonders that God has done which are so many that they cannot be recounted. He notes there was no requirement for any sacrifice. David notes his desire to do the will of God and proclaim righteousness to the masses.

Then David returns to the notion of needing the mercy of God, along with the love and truth, which have always protected him. After all, he still has troubles beyond count. He recognizes that his own sins have overtaken him. He therefore appeals to God to have those who seek his life to be put to shame and ruin and disgrace. he closes with the acknowledgment of being poor and needy and yet asking God to not delay for his deliverance.

Psalm 41

Psalm number 41 starts off with noting that the person is blessed who has regard for the weak. After all, God would never abandon such a person in times of trouble and also would protect such a person and preserve their life. God will bless that person and not give him up to the enemies. The Lord will protect such an individual from the desires of the enemy. In addition, the Lord will sustain them when they are ill.

His enemies are many and conspiring against him in whispering terms. Just like Job, even his closed friend, who he trusted and broke bread with has now conspired against him. David closes the psalm by appealing for mercy.

Psalm 42

The timeless beauty of this Psalm has been incorporated in hymns. The invoking of nature with the deer and the relaxing streams of water, combined with the metaphor of longing and panting for God, reaches its apex when we mention the soul thirsting for God. It is not merely God, though it is the living God.

Yet whether or not this psalm is written by David, it certainly has the overtones of his signature. Immediately after this wonderful opening he turns to the notion that he has been living and sustained on tears, because people have tormented him and asked him where is God in his time of trouble. He pours out his soul by reminding the listener in this Psalm, how he used to lead the multitude and procession to the house of God with joy and thanksgiving.

Then he raises the rhetorical question to his own soul, of why his soul is so downcast, and so disturbed. He rallies himself by noting that he will put his help in God. He will recall former accomplishments that God has done for him. He begins what seems to be his usual closure with additional poetic metaphors of the deep, calling to the deep in the roar of waterfalls. Then he returns to his lament before his final close of reminding people to put their hope in God, who is after all his savior.

Psalm 43

Psalm number 43 is another vindication, woe is me, bail me out God type of Psalm. Yet David gives God credit for being a stronghold, but in the same sentence raises the rhetorical question of why God has rejected him. David then makes a conditional bargain with God in which God will send light and faithful care and guide David to the holy mountain. Then he would go to the altar of God with joy and delight and praise.

Psalm 44

Psalm number 44 starts out very strong and maintains the recognition of the power of God for a solid eight verses. The exploits of God from day is going by our noted and repeated praise. By the time we get to verse nine however we once again have the feeling of rejection and retreat before the enemy. Indeed, David feels disgraced. David maintains that this happened despite the fact that he and the people have not forgotten God, or been false to the covenant. accordingly, David concludes this song by appealing to God to wake up and stop rejecting the people of the covenant.

Psalm 45

The author of this Psalm notes that he is writing for a King, which suggests that it is not David. He claims great skill as a writer. He knows that God has blessed the king with grace and blessings forever. There is then the Irish blessing with curses upon the enemy. Then, for some reason, the author of this Psalm goes into a story about young women being brought to the king in all their beauty. Interestingly, such women are virgins, but all their accompanying friends are virgins.

Psalm 46

Psalm number 46 starts out strong with recognizing God as refuge and strength. This leads to peace of mind. We always have our suspicion that the author has some personal gain at risk here. There is no such evidence of that though in this psalm. Yet there are some nice platitudes in this brief psalm, including the statement, be still and know that I am God. This is indeed one of the few psalms thus far that does not have any significant negative elements to it.

Psalm 47

Psalm number 47 continues the positive streak without negativity. There is much praise and clapping for the awesome God who has subdued nations. Indeed, God reigns over the nations, and is greatly to be exalted.

Psalm 48

This Psalm will continue the positive streak. There is again much praise and acknowledgment of the accomplishments of God. The forces of God are able to withstand the forces of many kings joined together.

Psalm 49

If we are prone to think of David as a prototype in forerunner of the Christ, then we may have some problems with this particular psalm. Granted, things may be pulled out of context on either side of the ledger. However, for the little list, we have a statement that no one can redeem the life of another, or give to God a ransom for them. If such a statement was followed to the extreme than many Christians would question your faith in Jesus Christ, who did exactly that.

Psalm 50

Psalm number 50 presents itself as an oracle of God. Indeed, God will not be silent. The heavens, themselves proclaim the righteousness of God and God's justice. That god of justice then proceeds to announce that he will testify against Israel. Nonetheless, there are no charges to that nation regarding sacrifices. God tries to distinguish himself from the anthropomorphic representation, and yet we still have that image of hunger.

The attempt to elevate above, and beyond the primordial type of god and anthropomorphic type of god, is also recognized when the oracle says to sacrifice thank offerings to God, and to fulfill your vows. God wants to be called on in times of trouble, and will deliver the faithful. This is the exact opposite with the wicked person. God notes that he has temporarily ignored people slandering their own family. There is perhaps in the next statement, a precaution of thinking that God is like us or vice versa. Perhaps this applies not only to the ancients but to us as well.

Psalm 51

This Psalm begins with a request for mercy, and to have transgressions and iniquities blotted out and washed away. After all the author knows, his sins are always before him. Nonetheless, somehow, he has sinned only against God. This psalm perpetuates the notion that people are sinful at birth even at conception.

There are some hints of deeper, thinking in this Psalm, when the author requests that God create the pure heart, and renew a steadfast spirit for the individual. Restoration is requested along with joy and salvation, and a willing spirit that is sustaining. Then perhaps we recognize that the author did not merely sin against God, but against a fellow human being with bloodshed.

Then we have the ambiguous closing of this psalm, in which the author notes that God does not delight and sacrifice or burnt offerings, and therefore, the authors sacrifice is a broken spirit and a contrite heart. However, immediately, after this, we have the very materialistic request to rebuild the walls of Jerusalem, so that God will, then delight in the sacrifices and burnt offerings with the notion immediately preceding this that they were not necessary.

Psalm 51 Expanded

Psalm 51 is a confession and mercy request by David. We are told in the headings that this psalm is inspired by the encounter between Nathan and David after he has committed adultery with Bathsheba. David seemingly puts it all on the line in the first verse asking for mercy from God according to the unfailing love of God, and the compassion of God. With this power, David feels his transgressions can be blotted out, and his iniquity washed away and cleansed from his sin.

By verse four, though we begin to see the typical David that we have come to expect when things are not going well. In this verse, David notes against you, God, and you only have I sinned and done what is evil in your sight. For anyone with a superficial awareness of the story of Bathsheba would have to consider this statement as somewhat disingenuous. Indeed, in the story in which Nathan confronts David, the prophet tells a story that engages David's sense of justice.

Nathan elaborates on a rich man who stole the only lamb of a poor man in order to put on a feast. David is naturally wishing to be just and condemns the man whom the prophet Nathan is portraying in his story. One of the most poignant moments in all of biblical literature occurs when Nathan turns to David and says that you are the man. David then gets the connection. Given this revelation, it is difficult to conceive how David has not sinned against his general Uriah, the husband of Bathsheba. This seems so obvious, and yet there is more to the story.

David as a man who is labeled someone after God's own heart, and a foreshadowing of Jesus Christ, may have some additional demons to deal with. Let us turn to the following description: #1 He was totally innocent. #2 a powerful king sought his death#3 he resisted the temptation, even in challenging circumstances. #4 he was spied upon within his own circle. #5 he was betrayed and abandoned by those closest to him. #6 he was vilified #7 he was a servant who suffered #8 he died an ignominious death.

Most Christians will understand the above descriptions to fit Jesus Christ who follows in the lineage of David. While this may indeed be true, all of these descriptions actually apply to Uriah who was the husband of Bathsheba. Don't take our word for it. Check out the story. Please see our expanded version of this in David And Michelangelo, Heart and Stone.

Returning to Psalm 51 verse five we see that David tries to blame original sin by noting that he was sinful at birth. Yet David desires to be cleansed, and gives a number of metaphors to that nature. Then we have one of the platitudes that David is known for, when he says in verse 10 to create in me a pure heart, and renew a steadfast spirit within me. David is indeed willing to confess as long as God will restore David's spirit. David will then use this experience to teach other transgressors the ways of God.

David then makes a nice distinction between blood sacrifices and burnt offerings and the sacrifice of a broken spirit with a contrite heart. He knows that this is what God is really after. Nonetheless David has to work in one final angle in the closing 2 versus in which he notes that after that has been achieved that God will prosper the people that David is responsible for. Then, for some reason the God who did not need burnt offerings, and the slaughter of animals will delight in such again.

Psalm 52

This psalm seeks to make a distinction between the fallen king Saul, and David. Saul is accused of loving evil and falsehood. The prediction is that God will bring him down. Meanwhile, the righteous will see in fear and laugh at Saul.

David on the other hand is like an olive tree flourishing in the house of God.

Psalm 53

Psalm number 53 opens with a rather straightforward proposition in which the fool says in their heart that there is no God. This is straightforward enough as it is, but it detracts from the dilemma of those who claim that there is a God, but either do not seek such a God in their heart, or pretend that because they do not say there is no God that they don't act like that. The next line is rather ambiguous when it notes that they are corrupt and their ways are vile and that there is no one who does good. It is not clear if the they is the fool, or it is all of us because the last statement notes that no one does good.

The next section in verse two attempts to clarify this, that when God looks down to see if anybody understands or seeks God, the reality is that everyone has turned away to corruption. Meanwhile, such people are overwhelmed with dread. This is the type of dread, that the first acknowledged existentialist in the 1800s, Soren Kierkegaard wrote about. The psalm concludes with the notion that the people of Jacob and Israel will be happy when God restores them. Perhaps we moderns can improve on this by producing the state of contentment, and not waiting on what we think is our predetermined restoration by God.

Psalm 54

Psalm number 54 is another one of those short palms where David is in hiding and in fear and requests God to bail him out once again. Of course, he does what everyone does by giving an undesirable characteristic to his enemies, such as arrogant and ruthless and that they are a people without regard for God. Surely God would deliver anyone who was the antithesis of such an enemy.

Therefore, David wishes for the evil to recoil on anyone who slanders him, because after all God is faithful. David then makes a deal like Let's Make A Deal TV show by noting he will make a sacrifice of a free will offering to God and praise God 's name. However, like many of David's prayers, it appears to be contingent upon deliverance and triumph over his foes.

Psalm 55

This is another Psalm in which David is deeply troubled and distraught. He commands God to listen to him and not ignore David's plea. David furthermore is commanding God to answer him. After all, the enemy is saying something that David does not like. Normally we might think that David would invoke the notion that enemy is saying something bad against God but we don't see that. The real heart of the matter seems to be that the enemy is bringing suffering on David and assaulting him.

David has lost the comfort that he felt in Psalm number 23 and is at anguish with tears of death and fear and trembling and horror. David wants to run away to the desert for shelter much like Hagar did in the Original Testament preceding him. David then appears to make the righteous claim that if it was an enemy who was insulting him that he could endure it. Now the enemy has become his companion and even his close friend with whom he once enjoyed fellowship. Although this is a description that fits Jonathan, his close friend, we see no evidence of such in the scriptures elsewhere to support this being anyone that close to him. In fact, arguably Jonathan, who was a great friend of David, dies in battle because the mighty warrior David is in hiding during a major battle. This is, however, very characteristic of David to feel that everyone has abandoned him when he is on the run and being threatened.

David then asks for a curse on his enemies. He then makes a distinction that in contrast to his enemies he calls on God who does indeed save him. Like the prophets of Baal, he has to cry out through the morning, noon, and evening in distress. Unlike the prophets of Baal, though he claims to be rescued and heard. He points out that he is saved by the God of old who does not change. David wraps up this psalm by pointing out how God will bring down the wicked and deceitful and meanwhile David will continue to trust in God. Indeed, if David were putting his motto on the dollar bill, he would say that in God we trust as long as such a God will destroy my enemy when I'm in hiding and on the run

Psalm 56

The key to Psalm number 56 as well as the key to all of David's philosophy may be summarized in verse three of psalm 56. There we see David, noting that when he is afraid, he puts his trust in God. Indeed, we do wonder where David is when things are not going well. For that matter, we find our answer by returning to the first verse, where David is once again requesting God to be merciful, when he is being pursued by his enemies. Later on David reminds God that he praises the word of God and trusts God, and is not afraid of God anyway. No, indeed, David is not afraid of anybody who has the power to rescue him, but he can sure display lots of fear from his enemies, when he is on the run.

David points out, that his enemies twist his words and formed conspiracies to take his life. David asked for a curse on them. If God will do this, such would be a sign that David would know that God is for him. We wonder if the converse is true, in the mind of David. David then gives once again some praise to God and asks the rhetorical question, what can men do to me if in God I trust and am not afraid. That, indeed, is a great question for David to ponder. However, David does not like to ponder on such questions, but does like to vacillate between fear and giving curses to his enemy and giving praise to God, as long as God will humor David and deliver him.

Psalm 57

This is another psalm of fear and hiding by David. We are told that this occurred when he was hiding in a cave from king Saul, who sought to kill him. David begins by asking for mercy because he takes refuge in God who vindicates him. Although David is in the midst of lions and ravenous beasts, God will send forth love and faithfulness on David's behalf. That way he can deal with the metaphor of men whose teeth are spears and arrows, and whose tongues are sharp swords.

David will then work in some exaltations for his God to be exalted above the heavens and have glory over all the earth. This brief interlude in verse five is followed by the description of what his enemies have done for him. David then reminds God that his heart is steadfast, and he will make some music for the occasion. He will tell everyone about the great love of God, including the people of all nations. Once again, he tells God to be exalted above the heavens. Indeed, verse five is the same as verse 11. This is a common framing of David, in which he frames his own accomplishments, along with his pleas to God by praise and exaltation.

Psalm 58

This palm begins with what appears to be a reasonable set of rhetorical questions about justice and equity. David then goes onto point out the injustice and wickedness of other people once again. What exactly would David want to happen to such people? David would like for God to break the teeth in their mouth and be like a stillborn child that never sees the sun. Somehow, this would make the righteous feel glad by being avenged. The ultimate sign of this is that the righteous will be glad when they dip their feet in the blood of the wicked. Unfortunately, this seems to be more than metaphor for David.

Psalm 59

Psalm number 59 starts out like so many of the psalms of David with request for deliverance from his enemies. Naturally, these enemies are evil doers. After all David has done no wrong. This time David does not want God to kill his enemies but keep them alive. Of course, the psalm must end with David praising God.

Psalm 60

In this, Psalm David knows that God has rejected them because God was angry. nevertheless, after giving examples of this, David closes this song with a statement that with God, we walk in victory and trample down our enemies.

Psalm 61

Once again, this psalm of David begins with a plea to God to listen. God is after all his refuge. The famous author of the 23rd Psalm or he will dwell in the house of the Lord forever, says in contradistinction to that, as he will no longer dwell in God's tent forever. However, David would still like to curry the favor of God and he requested God to increase the days the kings life, namely his own. He would like to be enthroned in God's presence forever.

Psalm 62

This Psalm starts out with some nice platitudes with David, noting that his soul finds rest in God alone, and his salvation comes from him. God alone is David's rock and salvation and fortress. Then we transition as often happens in verse three with David asking the question of how long God will assault a man. Then David returns to the same phrasing. He opened the psalm with. Finally, David closes this with a karma like statement that people will be rewarded according to what each has done.

Psalm 63

Psalm number 63 starts off in a typical fashion of David with using metaphors to describe his connection with God. This time, though he is literally in the desert. Still, he reminds God that David has seen God and his power, and knows of his love. David will praise God forever And will be eternally satisfied with the richest food. David remembers God in his sleep and clings to him because God's hand upholds David.

Now that we have the niceties out of the way, we can get to the real heart of the message in the last three verses. David goes on to note that those who wish to kill him will be destroyed. Not only will they die by the sword, but they will become food for jackals. Meanwhile while this is going on the king, that is David, will rejoice in God, along with all those swear by God. The people known as liars will be silenced.

Psalm 64

This Psalm is almost an inverse of Psalm number 63. With this Psalm, David begins with his complaints against his enemies. He suggests that they wait an ambush for innocent people. They also feed off of each other with her evil plans, and them covering up their plots of injustice. Even though such evil doers feel that they can hide from God David knows that they will be uncovered and struck down. Their own tongues and words will turn against them, and bring them to ruin. Of course, David must close with mention about how the righteous will be rewarded.

Psalm 65

This Psalm begins with praise, and has a hint of universality in it in which David notes that God will answer prayer and that all people will come to him. He also recognizes the tremendous power of forgiveness. At this time, David seems to favor election over free will, noting that it is God's choice to choose those who he brings near to his courts. Such a God shares the good things of his home and Temple along with righteous deeds.

The universality is recognized again when David notes as such a god is the hope for the ends of the Earth and the farthest seas. David then goes on to describe the majesty expressed by nature that represents God. David knows that God is a good steward of the land and protects such a land. David notes that the land itself expresses joy and gladness. His specific phrase that the hills are closed, but gladness is followed by the valleys shouting for joy and singing.

Psalm 66

David continues this Psalm with nature, expressing the joy and praise to God. He suggest that people come and see what God has done with his awesome deeds. Such a God will rule forever over all nations. There is again a suggestion of universality when David says for all people to praise God. This God protects and preserves life. To be clear David suggests that God does test people only to refine them. God may bring people to prison with burdens only to release them from their bondage. David closes this psalm by noting that the blessings of God would not have come about if David had not confessed his sin, but rather cherished that sin and his heart. However, David did confess and God delivered.

Psalm 67

Psalm number 67 may be an underrated psalm in terms of the church liturgy and utilization. There is a request for God to bless David and whoever the us reference is. We might naturally think that the us factor is on his own people, or even his own comrades and friends, but there is at least a potential for universality. Sure to say, though there may be a little bit of the virtue signaling when David opens with the statement, may God be gracious to us and bless us. Such a statement does not lend itself to suggest there is a direct request to God.

The next verse, though clarifies that in that David is speaking to God, so that the ways of God may be known on the earth and the salvation to all nations. Perhaps that is some clarity for who the us is from verse one. David notes that he wishes that all peoples might praise God. He adds to the universality concept by noting that nations are involved and may they be glad and sing for joy. Even before equity became the buzzword we have reference to such a concept in verse four. There is, perhaps some reference to stewardship with the land, yielding its harvest, and once again, closing with blessings, so that all people throughout the earth might fear God

Psalm 68

By the time we have come this far, we realize that David is not likely going to sustain themes of lofty notion. The first verse of this psalm makes it clear that he wants God to scatter his enemies. To be clear the implication is that they are the enemies of God But we know David and we know better. This is code phrasing for God, helping David to get rid of David's enemies. David may disguise this by using the analogies from nature of blowing his enemies away like smoke and melting them like wax but we know who and why here.

Now that we have that out of the way, it is time to sing praises to God, who is a father to the fatherless and the defender of widows and addresses the loneliness in families. God will release prisoners with joy. After all, God has a strong track record of delivering people when it looks bleak. By the way, God, you also provided for the poor and so you might as well keep it up and extend your blessings. Interestingly, this is one of the few psalms where there is a clear reference to women who are also going to proclaim the word of God. Arguably this proclamation by women may exceed the reference to men. The reference for women continues after kings and armies flea and leave behind the plunder. It is the women who divide the plunder.

We then see that David turns to more praise for God, and his ability to take captives and receive gifts from people, even those who are rebellious. David recognizes that his God is a God who saves and provides escape from death. Of course, this implies that God will crush the heads of his enemies, and bring them from the depths of the sea so that David and his companions can wade in their blood. Even David 's kingdom will have the dogs satisfied by the flesh of his enemies.

Now we will have a prolonged procession, recognizing the praise of God, and coming into his presence with such. God is requesting to summon his power and show his strength which rules over not only kings, but the beasts of the field. Yes, indeed, this is an awesome God, who will pass on some of that strength to his people

Psalm 69

We are told in the title that this is a psalm to the tune of lilies. Perhaps we get some clues in the first few verses, as to why David appropriated this tune. He asks for God to save him, because the waters come up to his neck, and then he's stuck in sinking in miry depths. So that we do not miss the water image he needs to include that two more times talking about deep waters and floods that engulf him. Perhaps he wishes to be like the water lilies, who though they may be in water still are very visible with their radiance.

David then identifies the source of the problems which are people who hate him without reason and seek to destroy him. David then goes on to acknowledge that he has some guilt that cannot be hidden from God. Then David begins one of those transitions where he starts by not wanting to make God look bad. He notes in verse six that may those who hope in you not be disgraced because of me and follows this with me those who seek you not be put to shame because of me. Verse seven will complete the subtle transition That David is known for in that first, David points out that he endures scorning, for god's sake, along with shame.

David then goes on to define how that shame has come into play in which he is a foreigner to his own family and a stranger to his siblings. Meanwhile, David of course maintains zeal for the house of God. By the way, God the people who intended to insult you have turned to me as the middleman. This is of course, an attempt for David, to align himself more closely with God, so that God can bail him out for all of his enemies, and apparently even his own family. Yes, David is the subject of scorn, including even by drunkards.

Then David turns to the God for whom he has born God 's insults and praised him for favor with his great love and certain salvation. He returns to the water image of sinking in the mire. And repeating the exact order of the earlier water images, he goes on to include the deep waters and the flood waters. David then demands an answer from God, because God is good with love and mercy. He demands that God rescue him and deliver him because of his foes. Yes, indeed, David is scorned, disgraced and shamed and helpless. All he was looking for was a little sympathy, but found none.

Perhaps David is not certain how God will respond to such request. Therefore, he goes on to do his version of the Irish curse starting in verse 22. He wants the table that is set before them to become a snare for their eyes to be darkened, and for the wrath of God to be poured out on them. He wishes for them to be forsaken and for their homes to be empty. Then David notes that God hurts people and wounds people, but that these enemies persecute such which, by implication, they do not have the right to do. Accordingly, David wishes for them to be charged with crime upon crime apparently because they have intruded both on the territory of God, as well as human beings simultaneously. Some might respond that such is a description of Satan.

Now we come to the closing stretch starting in verse 29, where David afflicted and in pain and all appeals to the salvation of God for protection. David will then praise God's name and song and Thanksgiving. This will once again be more valuable than any animal sacrifice. Poor people will see this and rejoice. The heavens and earth will also praise God when this happens. The people of Judah will rejoice and return to their rightful position.

Psalm 70

This brief psalm might be called a hasten psalm. David mentions three times to God in this brief psalm to hasten or come quickly, or do not delay. After all, David is once again, being pursued by his enemies and needs God to bail him out. Of course, every God could use a little help with an Irish curse which David is quite adept at. In anticipation of both deliverance from his enemies and deliverance of the curse, David closes with gratitude for his deliverance. After all he is only a poor individual being pursued relentlessly, and without cause.

Psalm 71

This is another refuge Psalm by David. He wishes to not be put to shame ever, and calls upon God to be his rock of refuge to whom he would always go. With that is the request to give the command by God to save David because God is the rock and fortress of David. Of course, once again, those who pursue him are wicked and evil and cruel. David points out of his own personal record is one of hope in God and confidence since his youth. He backs us up further in verse five that it is actually from his birth, and even some reference to the mothers womb.

The return on investment for God is that David will praise him and be a portent to many. Now David will transition from the youth aspect to that of old age, and commend God to not cast him away when he is old, and when his strength is gone. After all, David 's enemies speak against him and want to conspire against him to kill him. He brings God into the equation by saying that his enemies have said that God has forsaken David, and therefore they can pursue him because no one will rescue him. Such accusers need to be put to shame and perish, according to the Irish curse that David delivers next.

Of course, we must have a classic line from David: but as for me, I will always have hope and praise you more and more and tell of God's righteousness and salvation all day long. Now David will return to his youth in which he knows that God has instructed him. David knows then that he will continue to declare the marvelous deeds of God even when he is old and gray. After all, David will proclaim to

69

the next generations, and keep the process going of God's mighty acts. And that righteousness reaches to the heavens, and is prescriptive for life, especially that of David. It also goes to the depths of the earth and everything in between. Accordingly, David will give praise to God through music and instrument and acquire the righteous acts of God, especially in regards to those who wish to harm him and shame him.

Psalm 72

This Psalm is an appeal for justice and righteousness. If God endowed the king with these traits, he will pass them on to the people. Nature will share in the prosperity, and give back to the people the fruits of righteousness. Such a king will defend the afflicted people, and save the children of the needy. His kingdom will last as long as the elements of nature, such as the sun and moon. Other nations will bow before him, and serve him. The implication is that such a king will deliver the needy and afflicted even from other nations. When all of these things have been done by God through David, then it will be time to praise God.

Psalm 73

We might call this Psalm a surely Psalm. David uses the word surely three times in this psalm. The first two of these may be seemingly contradictory. In the opening verse, David says that surely God is good to Israel, and to those who are pure in heart. However, in verse 13 he says that surely and Van have I kept my heart pure, and in vain have I washed my hands in innocence. Those type of contradictions occur frequently in the Psalms attributed to David.

The third time we see the word surely mentioned is in verse 18 where David notes that surely God has placed this generation of his children on slippery ground, and cast them down to ruin where they may be suddenly destroyed. returning to the front portion of the psalm, we see that David envied people actually who were arrogant and prosperous, despite being wicked. Can you tell that such people did not have any struggles, and that they were healthy and strong and free from the burdens common to man. Yes, he notes that such people are prone to violence. David notes that such people are carefree with their wickedness and that they continue to gain wealth either despite this or even because of it.

David comes full circle starting in verse 21 when he notes that when his heart was grieved and his spirit embittered that he was senseless and ignorant like a beast. Nonetheless David was always with God being held by his hand. Accordingly, David will be guided and taken into the glory of God. He will indeed be in heaven, and will need no one else, but God who is his strength and portion forever. While the people who are far from God will perish, David will be near God, who is his refuge, which David will vocalize to other people.

Psalm 74

This is one of the rejection psalms by David. He claims that God is angry, and in fact has a smoldering anger. David feels compelled to remind God that he has purchased the people of Israel and redeemed them as his inheritance. By the way, God, our enemies have destroyed your sanctuary where you used to meet with us and set up their own signs and standards. At the end of this diatribe, David asked the question of how long will the enemy mock God.

David then goes on to tell God that God has been his king and salvation to himself and all of the Earth. He describes the power of God and majesty of God. He notes that God rules over all nature including day and night. Even the seasons of summer and winter are ruled by God. after this reminder, David has to remind God once again, how the enemy has mocked God and reviled his name. David reminds God that God has a covenant. This includes the oppressed and poor and needy.

Psalm 75

Psalm number 75 is an apparent song of Thanksgiving. David wishes to tell of the wonderful deeds that God has rendered. Only God is worthy of bragging as opposed to the arrogant and wicked, who boast inappropriately. Nobody can exalt a man, except for God alone. God can bring down or exalt an individual. nonetheless, David feels in the closing verse 10 that God might need a little bit of help and so he says that he will cut off the horns of all of the wicked while those of the races are lifted up.

Psalm 76

This psalm starts out with some sectionalism favoring Judah or Israel or Zion. This is opposed to the occasional Universalism that David describes. He gives God credit for destroying the instruments of war. He notes that such a God is resplendent with light and more majestic than mountains. David notes that God alone is to be feared. Then in verse 10, David makes a peculiar statement that surely your wrath against men brings you praise. Such a God is capable of instilling fear in kings, and breaking the spirit of rulers.

Psalm 77

The Psalm is it another plea for help by David. It is a reminiscence of times where God was in David 's camp. David is groaning as he remembers God and meditates noting his spirit is faint. Then in the middle of the night, David records his songs and he returns to meditation and reflection. Still the perpetual question in this psalm is will God continue to reject him and not show him favor as he has done in the past.

David then goes on to ask a question that is reminiscent of that from his predecessor Abraham. When Abraham is getting ready to destroy the evil sins of Solomon and Gomorrah where one of his relatives lives Abraham asked the question shall not the judge of all the earth be righteous. So too does David ask has God's unfailing love vanished forever. Has the God's promise failed for all time. Has God forgotten to be merciful. Has God in his anger withheld his compassion.

These are some pretty bold questions for someone in trouble. Then David catches himself in thought, and appeals to the times past when the Most High stretched out his right hand. David, because of the miracles of God and his mighty deeds. then goes on to outline the display of that power including the ability to redeem his people. He reminds God of the connection of Jacob and Joseph and later, Moses and Aaron. In between he notes the majesty of God, in the waters, in the clouds, and the thunder.

Psalm 78

This Psalm begins with a request to hear the words of David, who revealed things in a parable that have been hidden. Then he mentions that it is a parable before finally noting that it is an actual history lesson that he wishes to perpetuate for posterity. David then goes on with his history lesson to reveal the exploits of God in miraculous fashion over time deceived the people of Israel even after they had rebelled.

Then there is vacillation between David, acknowledging the sins of his ancestors perpetrated, and an acknowledgment of God's actions in the past. His depiction recalls the recurrent nature of God's people sinning against him, despite wonders performed by God. He details the fury of God when people questioned his ability to perform and care for his people. David is very descriptive of this. In verse 47 where he describes God's anger, his wrath, his indignation, and hostility. Then in verse 65 David suggests that God awakened, as though from a slumber, or like a man who is stuporous of wine.

All of this cycle of wondrous deeds performed by God, followed by rejection and failure to recognize and appreciate that wonder, followed by the indignation of God comes to a combination starting in verse 68. There we have the description that God favors the tribe of Judah over the other tribes, and built his sanctuary that he established forever. With that he chose David as his servant, taking him from a humble shepherd of sheep, in order that he made shepherd the people of Jacob with the integrity of his heart and skillful hands.

Psalm 79

Psalm number 79 is an appeal to God to deliver his people because other nations have defiled God's holy temple, and shed innocent blood of those who supported God.

Accordingly, David asked God if he will be angry forever. He requests that the sins of the past not be held against the current generation. God is challenged to get busy and save his people because otherwise the persecuting nations will say that God is impotent. The payback for such violation needs to be 7 fold according to David. Then David closes with the sheep metaphor and the promise of praise upon deliverance.

Psalm 80

This is another psalm of request for deliverance. The David question is how long will God be angry. He accuses God of making his people an object of derision. Following that, David demands that God restore his people as in times past. Then he follows with more accusations against God's destruction. After the description of that destruction, David makes an appeal to God for restoration which is an if then proposition. If God deliverers, then this time the people will not turn away.

This psalm begins with a request to hear the words of David, who revealed things in a parable that have been hidden. Then he mentions that it is a parable before finally noting that it is an actual history lesson that he wishes to perpetuate for posterity. David then goes on with his history lesson to reveal the exploits of God in miraculous fashion overtime deceived the people of Israel even after they had rebelled.

Then there is vacillation between David, acknowledging the sins of his ancestors perpetrated, and an acknowledgment of God's actions in the past. His depiction recalls the recurrent nature of God's people sinning against him, despite wonders performed by God. He details the fury of

God when people questioned his ability to perform and care for his people. David is very descriptive of this. In verse 47 where he describes God's anger, his wrath, his indignation, and hostility. Then in verse 65 David suggests that God awakened, as though from a slumber, or like a man who is stuporous of wine.

All of this cycle of wondrous deeds performed by God, followed by rejection and failure to recognize and appreciate that wonder, followed by the indignation of God comes to a culmination starting in verse 68. There we have the description that God favors the tribe of Judah over the other tribes, and built his sanctuary that he established forever. With that he chose David as his servant, taking him from a humble shepherd of sheep, in order that he made shepherd the people of Jacob with the integrity of his heart and skillful hands.

Psalm 81

This is a Psalm that begins with joy and praise to God for deliverance. David then transitions to an unknown voice as he describes it that is responsible for removing burdens. This unknown voice transitions further into the voice of God where David employs the God voice to quote the first commandment of having no gods before the supreme God. Then that God voice points out the people would not listen. Yet even as this God voice turns over his people to their own devices, he still points out that he would rather rescue them.

Psalm 82

This brief Psalm has several different elements to it. It begins with God in charge of the great assembly and giving judgments among the other gods. Then there is the rhetorical question which seems to question or challenge God by asking, how long will you defend the unjust and show partiality to the wicked. Then we transition to a command to God to defend the weak and the fatherless, and the poor and oppressed and the needy all from the wicked people. Then there is the ambiguity which follows saying that they know nothing and understand nothing and walk in darkness. It's not clear if that's all the oppressed people or the wicked people. Then we have the strange combination that says, that people are gods and the sons of the Most High, but will die like mere mortals and fall like every other ruler. This psalm closes by recognizing God is in charge of the earth, but challenging him to rise up. There is an element of universality where it is noted that all nations are his inheritance.

Psalm 83

This Psalm is another request, or perhaps even command for God to not be silent or quiet or still. After all, God's enemies and foes are plotting against God's people of Israel. They have all formed an alliance. There is a request to do what God has done to such evil people in the past. Such people are to be ashamed in this mood and perish in disgrace. Once again, David frames this like an Irish curse. Of course, he needs to close with reminding God that he is the Most High over all the earth. Basically, God needs to get busy and do what he does for his people

Psalm 84

This Psalm has a higher ratio of praise and adulation, as opposed to request and mercy. David begins this Psalm by noting how lovely is the dwelling place of God and David's desire to reside there. God takes care of the sparrows which is echoed in Jesus sermon on the mount. The only request seems to appear in verse eight where David requests that the God of Jacob look on the shield of Israel and guard his anointed one which is namely, David. David then utters the platitude that better is one day in your courts than 1000 elsewhere.

Psalm 85

David has already established that he cannot write too many Psalms back to back without a heavy request and plea to God. In this psalm he begins by pointing out how God has shown favor to Jacob and his offspring previously and forgiven people's iniquities and covered their sins. David acknowledges the wrath of God and how it was turned away. All David is asking for is to be restored again by the savior God who is to put away his displeasure from David and his people.

David continues his request by the rhetorical question of asking how long God will be angry with his people and wondering if it is going to last for generations. After all, if God revives such a people they will rejoice in the Lord God. The love of God is unfailing and with salvation. David then reminds that God promises peace to his people indicating it's somewhat conditional if they are faithful and don't turn to folly.

Psalm 86

This is another Psalm of supplication, or in other words, a needy Psalm four David. David claims that he needs protection because he has been faithful and trusted in God and deserves mercy. After all, he has been calling on God all day long and feels that he deserves joy, because he is the

Lord's servant and trusts in God. David senses that he has been alienated, perhaps because of some deeds and claims that God is forgiving and good and abounding in love and merciful. After all, David calls on God in distress because God answers him.

David has to say that among all of the gods out there in the universe, there's just nobody like the Lord God, and nobody whose deeds can compare to the Lord God. There is another element of universality in which David declares that all the nations created by God will come to worship him, and bring glory to his name because of his marvelous deeds. David knows that he needs to be instructed in the ways of the Lord and his faithfulness. David needs an undivided heart which will praise God because of his great love towards David.

Now we get to the heart of the matter and why David needs special favors from God. After all arrogant foes are attacking David and ruthless people are trying to kill him who have no regard for God. But you, of course, God, are a compassionate and gracious God and slow to anger and abounding in love and faithfulness. How about a little bit of mercy here, God, and show your strength if you have any left on behalf of your servant. Save me just because I serve you just like my mother did. This is one of the few times that David throws in the mother clause.

Psalm 87

This is one of those God likes us better than you psalms. This is all about Zion, and how it is favored other over other dwellings of Jacob and over other foreign cities, which have to acknowledge the place of Zion. After all the Most High,

Lord God will establish her, and write down basically that anybody who is anybody was born in Zion.

Psalm 88

With this Psalm, David might claim some copyright infringement from Simon and Garfunkel in the song The Sounds of Silence. After all, we can recall in that tune, hello darkness my old friend. The close of this psalm has David declaring that God has surrounded him with tears which destroy him like a flood and have completely engulfed him. God has taken David from his friend and neighbor. Darkness is his closest friend.

It is a bit strange that David starts this Psalm with attention to the Lord God, who saves him when he cries out day and night to him. Then David waivers slightly by saying may such attention to my prayer catch your ear, Oh God. Now for the heart of the matter is that David is overwhelmed to the point of death, without any strength left, and with 1 foot in the grave. He is like all the people that God has cut off from and will not remember. David is in the darkest depths. That is, indeed, why darkness is his friend. Indeed, he follows that statement that God has taken from him, his closest friends, and made him repulsive to them. David will turn one more time to the darkness image by asking if the wonders of God could be known in darkness, and in the place of destruction, or in the grave. Nonetheless, no matter how much David cries to the Lord for help, he perceives rejection from God who has hidden his face from David. David feels that he has been terrorized from his youth and close to death and destroyed by the terrors of God. Darkness is indeed the friend of David in this psalm.

Psalm 89

The start of this Psalm, and the end appear to be two completely different themes. However, these themes are very prevalent in David even though this particular psalm is attributed to another source. It is very much in keeping with the mood and themes and driving force of David. Realistically, one can turn to the motive of this Psalm by going directly to verse 46 there we have the David voice asking how long will God hide from him. Will it be forever. How long will the wrath of God burn?

David reminds God that his own life is fleeting. He accuses God of creating all humanity with a sense of futility because everyone is going to die and not escape the power of the grave. When one reads the first verse of this psalm, it seems like a forever psalm. That is David is singing of the Lord 's great love forever, that he will make known to all generations and repeating the same in verse two about the firmness and forever aspect of that love. It is a sign of heaven itself he notes there and a firm covenant so that we do not miss the forever theme. David continues this in the fourth verse.

David then goes into the sycophantic mode starting in verse five. There he notes that the heavens praise the wonders of God and his faithfulness. David raises the question of who can compare with the Lord who is in the skies. This appears to be a reference to the ancient sky gods, though, perhaps the sun and the stars and nature elements as well. Even in the council of the holy ones God is great, and he feared and more awesome than all who surround him. In addition to this, God is surrounded by his own faithfulness.

Next, the author of this psalm continues his recognition of the power of God, by turning to the earth and the surging sea that can be crushing, especially to the enemies of God. Yes, God owns heaven, but also earth, and all that is in it. Yet the author reminds God, that righteousness and justice are the foundation of your throne, along with love and faithfulness. Anyone who acknowledges this will be blessed and rejoice in the name of God day and night.

Next, we will turn to the vision portion in which the author wishes to convey a sense that God has spoken the words that follows starting in verse 19. He knows that he bestowed strength on the warrior as a young man in David, who is his servant and anointed one. That God voice will sustain David and strengthen him and not let the enemy get the better of him. That faithfulness referred to earlier now is bestowed on David and through God's own name will David's horn be exalted. Just as we saw that God ruled over the sea in earlier verses, now we have God setting David's hand over the seas and the rivers. Perhaps this is a little bit of one upmanship on God

In the ensuing section we are told that David will call out to God that you are my father, my God, the rock and Savior. God will then appoint David to be his first born, and the most exalted of the kings of the earth and maintain his love to David forever. Yes, keep in mind the forever theme of this psalm as we work our way to the conclusion. David goes on to recognize that, even with this forever aspect, through all his generations in offspring that his own offspring will be punished if they violate the statutes of God. However, God will not take his love away from him, or betray his faithfulness, or violate his covenant.

The God voice in the vision knows that once, and for all, he has sworn by his own holiness, that he will not lie to David, and that his line will continue forever and endure like the sun and moon and sky. How quickly the tide turns starting in verse 38 where the author notes that God has rejected and spurned his anointed one David, and been very angry and renounce the covenant that was supposedly forever. After detailing that downfall, we turn to verse 49 where the author asked God, where is your former great love which is your faithfulness that you swore to David. This calls to mind what the meaning of forever is in David's life and in David's time, and in our own.

Psalm 90

This psalm begins like many of David's with his sycophantic voice giving recognition to God as being the dwelling place throughout all generations well before the earth was formed. We have the platitude from everlasting to everlasting you are God in verse two. Another great platitude is uttered in verse four in that 1000 years in your sight are like a day that has just gone by. But then we turn abruptly in verse five to the concern David has that God is sweeping away people in the sleep of death.

David knows that they are being consumed by God's anger and terrified by his indignation. They don't even have the longevity of grass. Even if humans managed to live out their allotment of 70 or 80 years, they will still be set with sorrows and trouble and the like. David notes that the anger and wrath of God is as great as the fear which is his due. David tells God to relent and have compassion and satisfy the humans with his unfailing love. David believes the only fair compensation is to have as many good years as they had bad years.

Psalm 91

This is another psalm of refuge where David knows that whoever dwells in the shelter of the highest will rest in the shadow of the Almighty. Such a being will surely save people from deadly pestilence and their enemy. Such a person will no longer fear the terror of night. David knows that all anyone needs to say is that the Lord is my refuge, and then no harm will overtake you and no disaster will come near you. Then we have the verse quoted in the New Testament in reference to Christ where his angels will guard you in all your ways and lift you up in their hands so that you will not strike your foot against a stone.

Psalm 92

This is predominantly a praise Psalm as indicated in the opening verses. David will reference the love of God and proclaim it with music and singing. There is the anthropomorphic representation of God with hands doing work. There is also some great presumptions by David in claiming to know the thoughts of God and declaring those starts profound. he makes a distinction between his recognition and those of senseless people and wicked and evil doers. David reminds God that his enemies will perish and be scattered which is code language, or help me out here please God and do the same to my enemies.

Psalm 93

If we have a formula for David, not whining or complaining or beseeching God, when he is in trouble, it might well be represented by this psalm. This is only five verses long, and is full of praise with the recognition of the eternity of God, as well as his power over nature. What is more is that the statutes of the Lord stand firm also for eternity.

Psalm 94

After David has recited a brief Psalm that is basically of a positive nature to God, he returns to his usual ways. He is back to proclaiming God as an avenger, and a judge who will pay back the proud and the wicked and arrogant. These bad people slay widows, and foreigners, and murder the fatherless, claiming that God does not see such injustice. Such people cannot escape being detected by God because God can see into their minds and know their futile plans. David closes by noting that, even though the wicked band together that God will ultimately repay them for their sins.

Psalm 95

This Psalm starts off with very positive overtones, recognizing God as the salvation deserving of Thanksgiving and music and song. He is the king of all gods David notes as though some people believe there's at least something to those other gods. God is the master of the earth, with the mountains and the sea and the land. He is to be worshiped as though he is the shepherd and the people are the flock. Then we have a transition starting at the end of verse seven when there is a quote from God, referring to times past where the people of Israel tested God, even though they had evidence to do otherwise. There we are told that God was angry for 40 years. Because of those events, and or that anger, people were denied the entrance into God's rest.

Psalm 96

David continues a rare streak of mostly positive Psalms with this psalm of praise to the god of salvation. David wishes to declare his glory and deeds among all nations in all peoples. Such a God is to be feared above all gods. Once again, this does not dispel entirely the validity of other gods, but merely their hierarchy. However, in verse five, he does add that the gods of nations are idols.

David implies that these other gods cannot create the heavens or have majesty and glory for their sanctuary. Such a God is to be worshiped with offerings and prayers and a fear that trembles. This God will judge the earth and all the people with equity. Immediately, following the equity clause is that heaven will rejoice and earth will be glad. This concept of justice and equity is seldom mentioned in the scripture in which heaven and earth are on the same page. This is indeed, righteousness, as is noted at the conclusion of this song.

Psalm 97

David continues his positive theme of rejoicing because God reigns. This time, though we have some new imagery of not only clouds but thick darkness surrounding God. This is not incompatible with the righteousness and justice of God, which is the foundation of his throne. This God has a fire that consumes all of his foes. Lightning is employed for this effect, and even the mountains melt like wax before this God. This is, after all, the Lord of all the earth and heaven, and they proclaim his righteousness with a visible glory for all to see. Then we have a strange mixture in verse seven. The first part makes entire sense for the traditional belief system, in which people who worship images or idols are put to shame. However, why would we have the second portion which instructs all of the gods to worship the highest God? There is in this psalm, a bit of sectionalism favoring Zion and Judah, over other nations, particularly unfaithful and wicked people. God, meanwhile, causes his light to shine on the righteous.

Psalm 98

This Psalm continues the string of praise for the salvation of God, which is revealed to all nations. Immediately following this Universal declaration, there is the mention of a particular love and faithfulness to the people of Israel. Nonetheless, this is followed immediately by the notion that all of the people to the ends of the Earth have seen the salvation of God. This calls for tribulation with song and music. Nature participates in this joy with the seas and rivers clapping their hands, and the mountains also sing for joy. This type of God will judge people with equity.

Psalm 99

This is another psalm of recognition of the majesty and power of God. While there is some sectionalism, there is also some universality in which the author suggests that all nations are to pursue the greatness, and awesome nature of God. After all, this God loves justice and equity. There is a brief mention of Moses and Aaron. There is also the recognition that God punish the people of Israel for their missed deeds, despite forgiving them. Indeed, such a God is to be exalted above all other gods and people who tend to have a very difficult time forgiving those who have sinned against them.

Psalm 100

If David has a formula to increase his odds of being positive throughput a psalm, it is this: brevity. This 5-verse psalm has glad praise for God who created humans who belong to him. Humans are the sheep of his pasture. Thanksgiving and praise are due such a God who is good. What is more is that his love will endure through the generations.

Psalm 101

This psalm sings about the love and justice of God. Wanting to be in that camp, David extols the virtues of what his goals are. The first is to conduct business at home with a blameless heart. He does not need approval from the wicked but rather will hate what the faithless people do. He elevates some standards by noting that David will silence those who slander their neighbor in secret. David has no room for deceit- at least in others. As to whether or not he manages this for himself refer to our book David and Michelangelo.

Psalm 102

David's run-on positive Psalms was bound to come to an end. Indeed we gather that from the first verse when David is crying to God for help and telling God not to hide his face from him when David is in distress. David is an individual who likes to tell God to hasten his response, as he does in verse two. David's heart is withered like grass. He even forgets to eat his food because he is in so much distress. if one were to read the Scriptures looking for the word taunt, we would find that no one is taunted more than David. Not even close. David, of course brings this up often when he is being pursued by his enemies, often pairing this with the notion that God would not want his people to be taunted on his behalf.

By verse nine, David has forgotten that he has forgotten to eat, and is now eating food. Only it is eating ashes for his food and mingling his drink with tears. All of this is because of the wrath of God, which has thrown aside David. Indeed, David's days are like the evening shadow. Now that David's condition and perspective are in mind it is time for David to appear sycophantic. He wishes for God to be enthroned forever through all generations. He predicts compassion from God for Zion and David's people. After all, it is time for God to show favor to them. God will indeed answer the prayer of the destitute which is translated as David's people for the moment. David will have a brief relapse in verse 23 and claim that God cut short his days and broke his strength. Then he made supplication to God so that others might be honored in through all generations if God would restore him. After all, everything else will perish, except for God who remains the same and whose days and years never end.

Psalm 103

This is a solid praise Psalm from start to finish by David, which is somewhat a rarity. David calls upon his soul to praise God and his holy name. He calls to mind that this is a God who forgives and heals all diseases and redeems us from the depths of our despair. This God satisfies our desires with good things and keeps our energy like that of the youth and the ego. God is into justice for the oppressed the same God, who had been a terror to David in earlier songs is noted to be slow to anger abounding in love.

To be sure, David does acknowledge that God does accuse when he makes indirect reference to the notion that God does not always accuse as though he would sometimes. Then the anger comes back out of the equation that God is going to get angry, but just not forever. Nor will you give us exactly what we deserve for our sins. Yes, this God is a God of compassion compared to an earthly father, who has compassion on his children, so too does this God have compassion on all who fear him. Yes, this is an everlasting love to those who fear God, even the angels are to be part of this praise.

Psalm 104

This Psalm is another predominantly Praise Psalm, which brings in the role of nature as expression of that praise. this God has designed heaven and earth, with the waters in the clouds and the wind and flames of fire. Amidst all of the nature references is a positive reference to wine which warms the human heart. This seems to take precedence over even the bread which sustains those hearts. We have the juxtaposition that when God opens his hand all the creatures are satisfied with good things, but when he hides his face, they are terrified. When you take away their breath, they return to dust. This is then followed by the statement that when you send your spirit, they are created and renew the face of the ground.

Psalm 105

This is a praise Psalm with a history lesson. After beginning the Psalm with strong praise for the wonders that God has performed the author launches into a history lesson beginning with the descendants of Abraham. God made a covenant with Abraham that was to last for 1000 generations, or essentially eternity. This was followed up with Isaac, and then Jacob and Joseph in succession. We were told the travails and challenges that these descendants these descendants, and those who followed ran into. Sometimes these were of their own volition, and other times imposed upon them from the outside. In either situation, God continued to bail them out. In all these circumstances, he supplied their basic food and water. The Psalm is very much symmetrical closing with reference to the promise to

Abraham, and ending with praise, much in the same way that it began.

Psalm 106

This Psalm is another combination of praise with history lesson. Many of the same history lessons from the last Psalm are repeated here, but with a slightly different twist. Here the author points out that God continues to show favor to his people even after they had sinned. The author reminds God that he did this for his own namesake. There is an interesting turn in the pronouns, in which there appears to be a direct reference to God, with the pronoun, you're in which we see reference to the your miracles and your many kindnesses in verse seven.

Then, in verse eight, the God pronoun is changed here as though the author has gone from talking to God to talking to the people about what God did historically, in terms of bailing out the children of Israel through all kinds of adversity. This theme is repeated time and again, in which the people turn away from God only to return. Indeed, time, and again, we are told that the Lord was angry with his people, and withdrew his support only to return to his covenant pledge after he relented.

Psalm 107

This psalm begins with the very familiar words to give thanks to the lord, for he is good, and his love endures forever. Here we recognize that God has redeemed people in order for them to tell their story. This appears to have a universal element when we get to verse three when he talks about gathering the people from the east and west and north and south, including those who had wandered in the desert. There is a foreshadowing of Matthew 25 with the sheep and the goats, with being strangers, and being hungry and being thirsty, and crying out to God in their trouble who delivered them.

In the Matthew 25 sheep and goats' story, we have reference to the prisoners in a positive light. In this particular song, though we see a negative connotation about prisoners suffering in the dark other darkness in iron chains, because they rebelled against God's commands and the plans of the most high. However, even these people when they cry out in distress are saved from their utter darkness. We have another version of this when it comes to food, and which people rejected even food in their affliction, even unto the point of near death before they cry to God in their distress, and he saved them as well.

Then we have those who struggled at sea with the tempest and storms until once again, God heard them in their trouble and rescued them from their distress. This may well be another foreshadowing of Jesus in the boat with his disciples sleeping amidst the storm until they awakened him to calm such a storm. Finally we have the same theme in which people were in the desert and then became Blessed and then we're humbled and lost everything and finally once again, God lifted them from their affliction.

Psalm 108

This Psalm opens with praise and music to the Lord God, who is the greatest among the nations and higher than heavens, with his love and faithfulness, which reaches to the skies. Such a God is to be exalted with glory over all the earth. After David has given his glory, reference return to his ulterior motive in verse six, and which he appeals to

God to be saved, because after all, God loves them and has done so in the past as he references. However, he delivers a rhetorical accusation in verse 11, and which he says to God is it you God, who have rejected us, and no longer go out with our armies. David may not have the army that he needs to command for victory but he will command God to give him aid against the enemy.

Psalm 109

This is another woe is me Psalm by David. He opens this with a faint praise to God, and then immediately commands God to not remain silent. After all their wicked and deceitful people who have been impressing David with their lying, tongues and hatred without cause. A common theme is that such people have returned, evil for friendship and accused him wrongly. Of course, David responds that he is a man of prayer. Then he makes an interesting demand of God. He asked for someone evil to be appointed to oppose his enemy.

What is more is that David wishes for such an enemy to offer his own prayers which would condemn himself. He offers the Irish curse that may his children, the fatherless and his wife, a widow and his children be wandering beggars driven from ruined homes. Many creditors sees everything including strangers who will plunder him. he wishes this curse to extend to his offspring. However, even that is not enough as he requests the sin of such an evil person's mother to never be bloated out.

Then David request that God save him for God's names seek out of the goodness of his love, and to deliver him. After all, David is poor and needy and wounded. He requests that while the enemies curse that God bless and put the shame, his accusers and attackers. Of course, in exchange for this favor, David will with his mouth greatly extol the Lord and perhaps see fit to write a psalm or two like this one.

Psalm 110

This is an often quoted Psalm which begins with the phrase The Lord says to my Lord, sit at my right hand, until I make your enemies a footstool for your feet. then following this is the prediction that God will grant David, amazing victories over his enemies. David knows that the Lord has made an oath and will not change his mind. He quotes the saying from the Original Testament that predates him about Melchizedek who was a priest forever and that David will be like that.

Psalm 111

This Psalm is a praise Psalm, extolling the majesty, and works of God. Such a God does work that is faithful, and just and trust worthy. It is also eternal and rooted in faithfulness and righteousness. There is a redemption for the people that he has ordained in his covenant. We were told that the lord is gracious and compassionate, but somehow appears to provide food only for those who fear him. This psalm closes with another platitude, noting that the fear of the lord is the beginning of wisdom.

Psalm 112

This is another praise Psalm, but a blessing also to those who fear of the Lord. Since people will be rewarded with wealth and riches, and their righteousness will endure forever. Even in the darkness light dawns for them. Good things will happen to them because they are generous and lend freely and conduct their affairs with justice. The people also have a forever clause, in that they will never be shaken. They will have no fear and will triumph with success over their foes.

Psalm 113

This is another praise Psalm elevating God above all. This God raises the poor from the dust. The needy as well will be rescued.

Psalm 114

This is a brief history lesson about God helping the people Israel, especially coming out of Egypt. Because God is the ruler of the universe, and especially the earth, we are to tremble in the presence of the Lord, the God of Jacob.

Psalm 115

This Psalm begins with an unusual request that God's name in your glory, and not to the people. This is because of God's love and faithfulness. David is tired of having other nations ask where is their God. Meanwhile, the author challenges, the people of Israel to follow God. After all, there is a great blessing for those who do so.

Psalm 116

This Psalm opens with a conditional statement, in that David loves the Lord because the Lord heard his voice and heard the cry for mercy. The author is being threatened by the events around him, including the possibility of death. Meanwhile God delivers such people. because of all of this favor by God, David will fulfill his vows to the Lord, in the presence of all his people. David notes in this psalm that he is truly a servant of the Lord. He acknowledges that he had this passed on to him from his own mother.

Psalm 117

This is the briefest of all of the Psalms which focuses on praise to the Lord. Even in his brevity though, there is a universality, in which all nations extol the praise. After all, his love is great towards people, and his faithfulness endures forever.

Psalm 118

This is a Psalm of thanks. Indeed, we open with the familiar phrase. Give thanks to the Lord, for he is good and his love endures forever. There is a litany in which the people respond in kind with that phrase. Then the author knows that if the Lord is with him he will not be afraid, because what can mortals do. Even if all the nations arise against such a person, they will be cut down in the name of the Lord.

Psalm 119

In verse 18, we receive the perspective that compared to other psalms where David is requesting relief from his ordeals that this time, he has already had such relief. He knows in the past tense that God has chastened him severely, but not given him over to death. He then demands that the gates of righteous be open so that he can give thanks to the lord because God has answered him and become his salvation. We didn't have the well-known platitude that the stone the builders rejected has become the corner stone. No less than Jesus uses this statement as a reference to himself. Of course, the God who rescues people will go after the rejects. In fact, arguably, God goes only after rejects.

Psalm 120

This is another distress Psalm. David claims to be the victim of lies and deceit. David says woe to himself for living amongst such people of deceit and hate peace, which he himself is for.

Psalm 121

This is another familiar Psalm with the opening with the lines I lift my eyes to the mountains. Where does my help come from. The help comes from the Lord, who made heaven and earth, and will not let your foot slip. God himself will not slumber, but will watch over the people of Israel. The Lord is indeed the shade and will not allow harm from the sun nor the moon. This ever-present watch guard will watch over you both coming and going both now and forever more.

Psalm 122

This Psalm opens with a familiar verse in that I rejoice with those who said to me, let us go in to the house of the Lord. This is where the people of God gather. They also pray for peace and security, and for family and friends. David wants to make sure that he gets his ties into God, and knows that it is for the sake of the house of the Lord God that he seeks prosperity.

Psalm 123

This is a Psalm which begins by lifting up their eyes to God, and the heavens, in order to receive mercy. After all, the people of God have endured too much ridicule and contempt.

Psalm 124

With this Psalm, there is a recognition that if God had not been on their side that they would have been swallowed up alive, and swept away by raging waters. As it is, they escaped like a bird from the snare. After all, our help is in the name of the Lord, maker of heaven and earth.

Psalm 125

With this Psalm, we see that those who trust in God are like a mountain, that cannot be shaken, but rather endures forever. Then we see the familiar Irish curse of David, and what she says to do good to those who are good, but to those who turned crooked ways to be banished, along with other evildoers.

Psalm 126

This Psalm is a recognition of restoration, fulfilled dreams, and the like. Laughter and joy resound because of what God has done for his people, he knows that they went out, weeping, but return of the songs of joy carrying sheaves with them.

Psalm 127

This Psalm begins with another platitude, noting that, unless the lord builds the house, the builders labor in vain. This particular song is attributed to Solomon. There is a distinction here, compared to some of the Davidic songs in that children are mentioned as a blessing and heritage and reward, especially the children born in one's youth prayer. David on the other hand is big about the nonspecific forever generation clause being repeated time and again. Indeed, given the relationship that David had with his children, it is difficult for us to conceive of him writing this.

Psalm 128

This is another Psalm of blessings that does not appear to be that of David. The blessings after all, include the wife and children for the man who fears the Lord. Another uncharacteristic measure of the traditional Psalms is a blessing to see your children's children. We do not really recall blessed moments of David with his grandchildren. Also, this psalm does not mention any positive relationships with his children. We have expanded on that in our book David and Michaelangelo.

Psalm 129

This is a Psalm of oppression in which the author feels that he has been oppressed from youth. However, his oppressors have not gained victory over him. After all, the Lord is righteous and cut him free from the chords of the wicked. Then David finishes this psalm with an Irish curse that those people who have troubled him maybe turned back and put to shame. He also wishes to withhold any blessing that anyone else might give them who passes by.

Psalm 130

This is another plea for mercy. David knows that if God were to keep a record of sins that no one could stand before him. However, he finds God to be a God of forgiveness. David waits for the Lord with the vigilance of a night watchmen. After all, God will redeem the chosen people from all their sins.

Psalm 131

This Psalm is interesting, in that the author appears to be bragging that his heart is not proud and his eyes ate not haughty. Then he says that he does not concern himself with great matters or things to wonderful for himself. Then he knows that he is calm and quieter and so is like a weaned child and content. The conclusion of the people of Israel, putting their hope in the lord, is not congruent with the rest of this psalm.

Psalm 132

This is a request by David, to be remembered because of his claim to self-denial, and fulfilling his oath to the Lord. That is including not entering his house, or going to bed or sleeping until he found a place for the Lord and a dwelling for him. David requests that God come to that place, and for the sake of his servant, David, to not reject the annoy, namely David. Then we have the forever clause that David is so preoccupied woven into this psalm and where it is noted that one of the descendants will be placed on the throne. There is a conditional note that if those sons keep God's covenant, then they may have the throne forever.

Psalm 133

This Psalm opens with another platitude of how good and pleasant it is, when God's people live together in unity.

Several metaphors and historical perspectives are given to make this point. Hearing the term unity may not be universality, but it is a step in that direction.

Psalm 134

This is another very short Psalm, and consists entirely of praise. Indeed, if you want to find consistent positivity with David it is important for him to be brief.

Psalm 135

This Psalm is seemingly about praise as it starts with praise and ends with praise. Early on we get the praise of creation, followed by history lesson where God struck down other people for the sake of his chosen ones. There is a certain amount of our God is bigger than your God, braggadocio here. In the often symmetrical fashion of David, it closes with praise as well.

Psalm 136

This Psalm is a litany of giving thanks to God, for he is good for his love endures forever. It also indirectly acknowledges that there are other gods and other lords, but that this is the God of gods and Lord of lords, who does great wonders. It is the story of God's creation, which by verse 10 transitions into a God who destroys what he has created in order to protect his chosen people. He then sets aside the laws of the universe that he has created and divides the Red Sea, and does other miracles and more killing. Each one of these statements is followed by the statement that his love endures forever.

Psalm 137

The poetry of this Psalm, recognizing the spirit of captivity, was captured nicely in the play Godspell. There is a self-curse built into this song lest anyone forget Jerusalem, which is his highest joy. This song closes with one of the strongest vengeance statements in the Bible. After condemning the captivity in general, we have the closing verse that happy is the one who seizes your infants and dashes them against the rocks. If we must read this song metaphorically, we might will say that the opening A-side was quite good, but that the B-side closing should never have been produced.

Psalm 138

This Psalm is characteristic of many by David by opening with praise to the Lord, for his unfailing love and faithfulness. There is a bit of universality when he knows that all kings of the earth will praise the Lord for his glory is great. Nonetheless, David knows that this great and exalted God still looks kindly on the lowly. After we have the sycophantic flattery out of the way, David then tells God what to do to vindicate David and not abandoning the works of his hands. This follows the pattern characteristic in so many of the Davidic psalms in which the reader may go to the last line to obtain the ulterior motive of David at the moment.

Psalm 139

3/4 of this Psalm is flattery to God about how well God knows David and all of his inner thoughts and actions. He knows that there is nowhere that he could go that he could hide from the spirit of God, or in any way, shape or form hide from his presence. He knows that God saw all of David and his actions even before he created him. He attributes precious thoughts to God that are innumerable. Immediately after that statement, David launches in to the request for God, who is so great to slay the wicked, because after all, they speak of God with evil intent as though perhaps, God knew David well and his thoughts, but maybe not so much the evil people. David then goes on to note that he hates such people who hate God and are in rebellion. Finally, he challenges the same God, who knows all of his ways and actions and thoughts before he thinks them to once again search the heart of David and test him.

Psalm 140

This Psalm gets right to the heart of the matter by telling God what to do, namely to rescue David from violent and evil doers. After detailing the many ways that the evil doers act, David goes into one of his classic Irish curses. May the mischief of their lips engulf them, and may burning coals fall on them, and may they be thrown into the fire into miry pits never to rise. Of course, David has to close this by acknowledging that God will secure justice for the poor and needy and the righteous.

Psalm 141

Psalm 141 basically may be paraphrased hey God I'm talking to you and you need to act quickly in the opening lines. This characteristic Davidic psalm continues to tell God to put David's prayer before him and to set a guard over his mouth. He tells God to not let his heart be drawn to evil. He doesn't want any part of their delicacies. He even requests that he be stricken by a righteous man to be rebuked. Then David will make his prayer against the wicked. Instead, his eyes will fixate on God while the evil fall into their own trap.

Psalm 142

This is another Psalm of desperation as David himself declares in verse 6. Of course by the time this is acknowledged we see several other related descriptions highlighting this theme. Of course, another condition connected with this request is that the righteous will rally around him.

Psalm 143

This is another request for mercy by David. More properly it is a command by David for God to listen and act on behalf of his people. Of course, David deserves such favor because he meditates on all of the works of God. After his case is made David commands God to act quickly on his behalf. David has put his trust in God. Then he retreats a little from his perfection lifestyle position and asks to be instructed a couple of times. Of course, all of this would be for the Lord's sake.

Psalm 144

This Psalm starts off with praise but we know better than to believe such will be sustained. After some self deprecation of humankind, David gets to the heart of the matter. It is time for God to use his energy and natural power to scatter David's enemies. Once God has accomplished this, then David will sing a new song to God. Blessings will then come to the people of God.

Psalm 145

This appears to be predominantly a Psalm of praise that celebrated the abundant goodness and compassion of God. God is after all slow to anger and rich in love. There is a hint of universality in that God is good to all people and has compassion on all he has made as we read in verse 9. Indeed, all men will praise God praise. Yes God is faithful and keeps his promises. He hears everyone who calls on him. He even fulfills their desires. Of course, we have to work and alone towards the end that God will destroy the wicked and then David will speak in praise.

Psalm 146

This Psalm is 90% praise with some nice platitudes of not putting trust in mortal man. This God opposes the cause of the oppressed and hungry and prisoners and blind. He even watches over the alien and sustains the faithless and the widow. We do have to get that in a dig on how this God frustrates the ways of the wicked. Then we close once again with praise.

Psalm 147

This Psalm is seemingly a praise psalm that displays the natural wonders of God as illustrated in natural metaphors. However universal wonders of God may be though, this is a strong sectional work where the blessings are intended clearly only to the house of Jacob and not other nations who by interference from verse 6 are wicked.

Psalm 148

This Psalm is a rare praise psalm from start to finish. Praise comes from the heavens, sun, moon, starts, waters, and all of the earth. While it hints at universalism by having the kings of all the earth and all nations contributing to the praise, we see at the end that the true beneficiaries of this will be only the people of Israel.

Psalm 149

This Psalm starts off with flurry of praise. However, the ulterior motive is revealed in verses 6-9 which this psalm bears out. The purpose is to inflict vengeance on other nations.

Psalm 150

Psalm 150 is another rare praise psalm from start to finish. It's almost like it took David a long time to recognize this ability as 2 of the last 3 psalms are this way whereas this a rarity in the others. It is hard to argue against the final line that says let everything that breathes praise the Lord.

Psalms 119

Much has been written about the longest Psalm in the Bible, number 119. There are many elements consistent with those that David has submitted on other Psalms, even though he is not necessarily the author. These include his usual lamentations or woe is me verbiage. The Psalm is interspersed with praise and vindication. There are petitions for wisdom and the acknowledgment of disobedience. There are 22 sections with eight versus each representing a Hebrew letter. The song is a rather sophisticated acrostic by design.

In the first section, the author recognizes first of all that there is a blessing to be blameless, but then the acknowledgment that his own ways have not necessarily been blameless, and therefore he has shame. In the second section, he describes how hard he has tried to keep those laws. In this section we have the well known platitude that the stone the builders rejected has become the cornerstone. No less that Jesus uses this statement as a reference to himself. Of course, the God who rescues people will go after the rejects, in fact, God goes only after rejects as the nonrejected are already attracted to God. In the third section there is a request for God to be good to the author because he has obeyed the commands of God. With that is included a rebuke against arrogant people who scorn the author.

In the fourth section, we have the recognition of how the author has been humbled, despite giving an account of his ways. Nonetheless, he wishes to meditate on the wonderful deeds of the Lord and be kept from deceit. The fifth section parallels that of the fourth. In the sixth section, there is a request for the unfailing love and salvation that was promised to fall upon the author. In the seventh section there is a reminder to God to remember his servant and the promises made to him.

In the eighth section the author reminds God of the promises that he has kept for the sake of God. In the ninth section there is a request for God to be good to his servant and teach him knowledge and good judgment. It is one of the rare times in the Psalms that we see an acknowledgment that it was good to be afflicted, in order to learn from the Lord. The 10th section is a mixture of acknowledgment of his creator with the fact that the author has put his hope in the hands of the Lord. There is an appeal to the unfolding love and compassion of God. There is also a request to shame the arrogant.

In the 11th section, we see frustration about waiting for the fulfillment of comfort. After all, the author has not forsaken the precepts of God. The 12th section focuses on the eternal nature of God's laws. With that is a request for salvation because the author has sat the precepts of God in his heart who is both eternal and boundless. The 13th section focuses on how the author meditates all day long. He notes that such a process elevates him above the teachers and elders.

The 14th section begins with a familiar platitude that God's word is a lamp for my feet and a light on my path. The statues of God are with the author despite the traps that the wicked have set for him. In the 15th section we see the authors hatred for evil doers and double minded people, and an appeal to God to be address the challenges such people project. In the 16th section, there is an extension of this by an appeal to God to not be left to his oppressors, but to be dealt with according to the love of God. There is a request for wisdom and discernment in order to understand the statutes of the Lord, which he desires more than gold.

In the 17th section, we see once again how wonderful the statutes of God are which give light. There is an appeal for mercy and to be redeemed from oppression in order that the author might further obey the precepts of God. In the 18th section we see the justice of the laws of God, which are righteous and trustworthy. The author cannot forget these laws despite persecution and distress. In the 19th section, the author notes that he will call on God and will obey. if God will do his part, then the author will keep the appropriate statutes.

In section 20 there is another request for deliverance from suffering. After all, the author has not forgotten the laws of God, unlike the faithless who are disobedient. In section 21 we see the extension of the persecution to the author this time by rulers. Nonetheless, the author keeps his heart settled on the word of God and he detests falsehood. The author anxiously awaits his due salvation because of obedience to the commands. The final section 22 is a summary of the supplications of the author for deliverance. Yet the close of this long Psalm is a rare recognition that he has strayed and wishes to be sought out like a lost sheep.

PROVERBS

04-29-24

PROVERBS 1 TO 31

INTRODUCTION

Proverbs is an incredible Biblical book that documents human behavior by providing examples of behavior that should be emulated and those to be avoided. The contrasts between the good and the bad are usually very stark and sometimes the bad seems to have no redeeming value. But that contrast forces the reader to choose the good or the bad.

The structure of proverbs presents multiple behavior groups for review. These groups reflect the political, religious and social structure of the Solomon era. Despite the fact that Proverbs is an ancient book, the examples are very familiar and attributable to people and society today. Greed, injustice, dishonesty, and other improprieties are all described as well as the virtuous antidotes. Maybe human nature hasn't changed over the centuries, only the clothes and the trappings that define us.

But the important fact is that for every negative attribute, a positive value is also presented. The reader needs to make a choice: which one is me?

Another way of illustrating the choice follows:

You will find everything you want to do or be endorsed.
You will find everything you don't want to do or be rebuked.

Rich

PROVERBS COMMENTARY

When we decided to include Proverbs, we knew we would deviate from our formula of not using outside resources. The rationale was that all of our works to date provide adequate measures to reflect on without resorting to out-side measures. In this work we felt that Psalms has plenty to reflect on by virtue of the strong connections attached to David. Indeed, if on has read our other work on David and Michelangelo, then one can reasonably ascertain if a particular Psalm is connected with David and what was going on in his life at the time.

Ecclesiastes on the other hand does not need a connection with a strong historical figure to derive significant philo-sophical perspective from. While some may have liked to connect this with Solomon, aside from the evidence against that, it really won't help anyway, because we don't really have that much about Solomon's d his background. The precepts there are mystical enough to allow for speculation. Proverbs, on the other hand comes across fairly straightfor-ward for exactly what is written. It is hard to add anything unless one has a reference.

A friend who knew that we had already published 2 books on Job thought we might be interested in the work by Robert Alter the Wisdom Books. Indeed this gem brings much to the table because of the author's intimate knowledge of the language and history. While it not the type of measure that we wanted for Job, we felt it quite helpful for Proverbs. We used this modestly for Ecclesiastes for the background history. Since Alter referred often to the work on Proverbs by Michael Fox, we have included information from his work.

We will not make much of the notion that the order of Proverbs is not the historical order in which they were written. Proverbs 1-9 has been shown very convincingly to have been written later than the main body. While this may bear some importance for scholars and be referenced by us, we will still write our essays in linear fashion. We recognize that Proverbs is an anthology with poetry, wise sayings, dialectics, even satire and the like. All of these sayings are generally done with some system of mnemonics in mind.

The idea behind mnemonics then and now, is to render something more memorable. This may be achieved by rhyming schemes or alliteration, or other similar type of literary device. This becomes more essential when people do not have great access to written word or other recordings. Perhaps this very style influenced the presence of Proverbs in the cannon since it does not have a characteristic particular Israelite theme to it. Rather this work like other Wisdom books such as Job and Ecclesiastes may be appreciated by a more universal audience.

Steve

Proverbs – Chapter 1

The first thing that Alter notes after dismissing any significant consideration for Solomon as author of Proverbs is that this work means proverbs of. It is an artful expression which is not merely an anthology but is rather an anthology of anthologies. The term proverbs according to Alter can also mean parable, poetic theme and a rhapsodic utterance. There are repeated warnings for young men to heed in order to avoid the ravages of a shrewd woman.

If one wishes to increase their wisdom, then they need to understand riddles and parables we note in verses 5,6. In verse 7 we have a familiar platitude in that the fear of the Lord is the beginning of knowledge but there is a double distinction in the couplet that follows. There we are told that fools despise wisdom. This of course is a subtle twist in which knowledge has been replaced by wisdom. That is the real essence that a fool cannot do. This way of thinking is supportive of the people of Israel as favored.

Beginning in verse 8 we get the introduction of the mentor who instructs his young mentee to listen to his father and mother. This parallels other ancient writings such as the Egyptian. The mentor will have various warnings for the youth to heed. First is the literal bandit on the road, although there is the opportunity for metaphor here as well. Yet the instructor notes that ultimately the criminals will be apprehended by their own schemes. Indeed we have the statement in verse 18 that these men lie in wait for their own blood.

Next we have the introduction of wisdom. While some have used the proper name Sophia from the Greek connection, such cannot be derived from this reading or the most ancient version. It is even questionable if this wisdom is even consistently feminine as is often portrayed. Certainly later references support the use of the feminine However, as is interpreted in the New International Version there is a warning on rejecting wisdom that will parallel the admonition to reject the evil woman. Wisdom in turn, laughs at the misfortune of those who turn away. This chapter concludes with the notion of a payoff for heeding these sayings.

Proverbs – Chapter 2

Chapter 2 begins with a challenge for the student to reflect on the ways of wisdom for 4 verses before noting the payoff in verse 5. That payoff is understanding the fear of the Lord as well as finding the knowledge of God. This is a fairly radical transformation that begins with the implied position that the adept does not have much background in wisdom which is expounded on for 4 verses. Ah yes, but stay with the program. You will not only be imbued with the wisdom of the earthly master, but will also have the knowledge of God.

There is a lot of potential here in verse 5 where the end of the rainbow is this combination of fear of the Lord along with the knowledge of God. Fear does not sound like something we would aspire to even if it is fearing God. Perhaps we would do well to translate this as respect. We moderns can live with that translation and excuse that fear language as a bit of anthropomorphism. Perhaps we rationalize that if we have to fear God in order to have God's knowledge, that such trade off is worth it.

It is interesting to consider that we usually think of wise as a more worthy goal than knowledge. Indeed, the usual order is that we acquire lots of knowledge first. Then if we really are fortunate, we may obtain wisdom. Here the goal is reversed in that we are aiming for insight, understanding, and wisdom first and then we obtain knowledge. Of course, the knowledge of God would surely include wisdom we might postulate. Indeed, if God has all knowledge, is there a need to have wisdom, or is wisdom a mere subset of the knowledge of God?

Let's take a look at the first half of the promise to the successful adept. They will understand the fear of the Lord. Let's remove the anthropomorphic notion of some superpower that can do to humans whatever they do and so must be feared like a drunken father who might be lovable at times but unpredictably violent at times. Instead of the substitute term respect though, this time let's look at the ambiguity of the statement. The aim is to have the understanding of the fear of the Lord? Does this imply that God has fear?

Let's probe the possibility that God has fear. What would God fear? Perhaps we have a clue in one of our earlier works in which we see that Adam and Eve were expelled from the garden because God was concerned that they would have knowledge, as in the knowledge of good and evil, without the wisdom to apply it. The adept is promised that at the completion of their mentorship that they will understand that. They will understand literally the fear of God. Perhaps this is the type of fear that those involved with the first atomic bomb were experiencing.

The rest of this chapter is a combination of using that wisdom acquired to protect oneself by storing it in the heart which was the seat of understanding for the ancients as well as emotions. The failure to recognize this connection as moderns contributes to many health issues. Then the instructor begins with some general warnings to not forsake the path. This becomes a specific warning against seduction by a woman. The woman is married and not necessarily as commonly portrayed a foreigner. Rather what is alien in the circumstances is that the relationship is alien to what God has ordained.

Such a choice leads to death. This can be construed as death from disease, death by the hand of the husband of the seductress upon his return, death by psychological guilt, or death by the hand of God. This may be represented by a psychological death. Fox notes that one of the key source's notes that the woman in 2:16-20 is an allegory for all illicit counsel in the line of Midrash interpretation. Alter even points out that the Hebrew language makes a pun that to come into a woman means to have sex with her. In contrast, with survival of life on the line, it is the ethical person who survives and not the men who succumb to the seductress.

Proverbs – Chapter 3

This chapter begins with a promise of a reward if the student mentee remembers the teaching of the master along with his commands. Notice these commands are attributed to the teacher and not to God as though God benefits from intermediaries. The reward is prosperity. The implication according to Alter is that this is physical, longevity, along with possessions. The notion of hanging the precepts around your neck and writing them on the tablet of your heart demonstrates both an external reminder as well as internal. Fox notes that the rewards of piety are still to be considered as grace and not necessarily what we have earned.

Alter points out that verse 4 where the concept of good regard is used may refer to either intelligence or even common sense. Fox agrees with the root word here meaning to both see something and to understand it. Next we have the familiar platitude of "Trust in the Lord with all your heart and lean not on your own understanding "found in verse 5. The corollary follows in the next verse to not be wise in your own eyes. With this we are instructed to fear the Lord again. The promise for this is a healthy body and nourishment for your bones. Fox notes that verse 9 implies that our sacrifices must come from honest earnings.

Now we have a little more sophisticated second stage command. Earlier we learned that prosperity was itself a reward. Now after one has become prosperous, they are to once again honor the Lord with their wealth. There are echoes of this in the New Testament including the parable of the talents. Indeed, as noted here, such giving results in even more abundance. This is followed by another platitude that the Lord disciplines those he loves as noted in verse 12. Here the comparison is to an earthly father who would do the same.

The following verses which culminate in verse 20 shows the virtues and benefits of wisdom. Many translations have wisdom here as a female entity which may be more accurate here than the first chapter. Assuming this to be the case we have a co-creation in verse 19 where we note that the foundations of the earth were laid by the Lord through wisdom. In verse 20 Alter notes that we have a reference to the great flood when the author notes that the Lord divided the deeps (water) by his knowledge.

Next, we have different ways of depicting wisdom as in sound judgment and discernment. Those who follow this way have nothing to fear, unlike the wicked. This is followed by simple stand-alone individual recommendations. Don't withhold good from those deserving. Don't put off your neighbor in need, don't plot against your neighbor, don't accuse anyone for no reason. Don't envy a violent person. God will mock and curse violators of these precepts and bless those who keep them.

Proverbs – Chapter 4

Chapter 4 begins with the instructor telling his sons to pay attention to his instruction. This becomes perhaps more precious when we realize that the instructor was an only child whose parents would have given him anything that they could have. They chose to emphasize the learning to achieve wisdom. Here Alter notes again that wisdom is represented as feminine. This wisdom is protective but itself needs protection. This wisdom is worthy of any price even if it costs all that a person has.

The next section begins with a promise of long life if the wisdom imparted is heeded. The student is to guard this instruction with his life. This is food for the soul in contrast to the wicked whose sustenance is the bread of wickedness and the wine of violence. Alter agrees with Fox on the interpretation of the light metaphor as the moment when light is fully risen but in contrast to Fox who suggests that it means dawn. Either way this is in contrast to the wicked whose way is the direct contrast of deep darkness.

A new section begins with an admonition playing off the previous section where light gives sight. This time the command is to not let the words of wisdom out of sight. Rather they are to be kept in the heart which the center of understanding or even conscience. The adept is to keep his eyes from perversity and corruption.

Proverbs – Chapter 5

This chapter is filled with metaphors and admonitions revolving around the notion of avoiding the seductress who is probably another man's wife. The instructor advises that the student's lips preserve knowledge rather than fall pray to the seductress whose lips drip with honey. That sweet taste and smoothness turns to bitterness and leads to death. Paying her a visit robs one of their strengths and even life years. This pathway allows others to enjoy your wealth which is a common lament in Ecclesiastes.

Such an individual who does not heed this discipline will groan prematurely that their flesh is spent. One can almost read into this a venereal disease. Drink your own well water because it is reliable. Yet those springs of life's essential element are to be protected and not shared. The commandment here is not meant to be an admonition to avoid sharing but rather a metaphor to neither share your wife or to take a share in another man's wife. Fox adds the notion that the author meant to show the question of linage when one sleeps around as well as the disadvantage of a male not being able to raise his offspring in his own home. Returning to the light and visibility factor from the previous chapter we see that all one's actions are visible to God.

Addendum:

Fox points the many possibilities of meaning of the sexual unions in chapter 5. Various versions treat the sexual unions as allegories for spiritual unions rather than mere sexual unions. However he cites evidence of the positive blessings of a large family. Fox notes the importance of being open to a playful exchange on the misuse of words in the sexual context. We moderns might feel that we can readily distinguish between the seduction of the evil mistress and the good female Wisdom. It takes a person paying close attention as well as knowing the nuances and avoiding our preconceptions to render a proper understanding.

Proverbs – Chapter 6

This chapter opens with practical advice to avert financial ruin. Don't guarantee loans for others. Our words can entrap us we are told so work to free yourself. This may require some humility in regards to that neighbor. Even an ant is not sluggish at doing what needs to be done. Despite no leadership, it gets the job done. The teacher goes on to note that the corrupt mouth of the villain along with his winking eye, foot signals, and hand signals are gestures associated with seduction or deception according to Alter.

Then in verse 16 we have a serious things we are told that God utterly detests. First we are told there are 6. Immediately after that we are told 7. Then the list is given and it is actually 8. Fox points out that this may be either scribal error or rather as a representation of concept rather than accurate number. The point is here that a literary device is employed to make us pay attention. Most people will not actually count them but by being given a number, may pay better attention. Lying, haughtiness, scheming, false witnesses, and those who shed innocent blood showcase the list.

Then the teacher goes into another unit that warns against seduction by an adulteress. The safeguard is to bind God's teachings around your heart and around your neck. That is an external visible reminder along with something written on the heart. Those who fall prey to the seductress are reduced to a loaf of bread. The fool who plays with such fire will burn his lap and clothes. Such an individual has probably not taken Tony Robbins fire walk and will be burned by the hot coals that they walk on.

All of this is contrasted with a thief who steals to satisfy his hunger. He will be caught and pay a heavy restitution. So, it is with a man who commits adultery. He will be publicly shamed. What is more is that the jealous husband will show no mercy no matter what bribery is offered. Fox notes that the message was meant to convey that what a thief steals could be restored but not so the actions of adultery whether disease, offspring, or reputations.

Proverbs – Chapter 7

Proverbs chapter 7 is a narrative poem from start to finish. There is the usual up front exhortation for the student to keep the master teacher's commands by guarding them with the apple of the eye and writing them on the tablet of the heart. Yet the teacher knows what can derail a young man which he begins to detail in verse 6 where he looks out from his elevated window to see an at-risk young man among the other young men.

What is it that distinguishes this young man from the other men? He lacks judgment. The youth is going near the corner of her house as though we are supposed to know who the female reference is. As darkness descends literally we see darkness falling on the young man as he is greeted by the woman. She is dressed like a prostitute and has a crafty intent. It is important here to note the distinction of this woman. She is not a prostitute. Indeed for all the warnings in Proverbs they do not appear to be about prostitution.

We will not go so far as to say that either the teacher or that Proverbs itself condones prostitution. However he does not feel that such practice warrants the same precaution or derailing potential that this situation does. She is instead a married woman whose deception is that she masquerades as a prostitute. She is loud and defiant we are told. Who is she defiant to? Perhaps this is a distinction from a typical prostitute who would normally be accommodating and not defiant. Then we are given a strong clue.

Her feet never stay at home. She has a home and a husband. She is aggressive physically towards the young man. She is disingenuous when she says that she needed to fulfill her vows with fellowship offerings at home and now can have a liaison with the young man? Has she satisfied her husband and so now is free to engage with others? Alter points out that this is a combination of hypocrisy in being sexually assertive right after coming from the temple, but also that she will offer him a meat dish before he feasts on her.

She takes him to a well adorned well prepared couch. Alter notes that the linguistic interpretation here that follows is this offering the young man a night of continuous sex. She spells out that her husband is a on a long journey and will not intrude. He is a successful businessman gone for up to a month or so. Then the seduction is spelled out with strong metaphors like an ox going to slaughter or a deer stepping into a noose, or a bird in a snare. The teacher summarizes a strong warning not to join the ranks of the many who have been seduced.

Proverbs – Chapter 8

In the last chapter, we saw that the story within a story involved, looking out from above at someone who had chosen a lower pathway. Now we will have a clarion call from wisdom and chapter 8 looking out once again from the highest point. The message here is that Wisdom, unlike the dark side of life is not hidden. It is available to anyone who listens. In fact, the universality is recognized in verse four in which wisdom voice is raised for all humankind.

In fact, we see that wisdom does not give up on even the simple minded or the foolish as we note in verse five. There is still time for such people to acquire some insight by paying attention to wisdom. The teacher then goes on to note that his disclosures are trust worthy, and in contradistinction to wickedness, whose ways are crooked and perverse. The notion that such wisdom is available to all who are discerning is once again evidence of the universality of this particular section.

Next, we get some relative value scaling of the position of wisdom. It is indeed more precious than rubies, and beyond anything a person can desire. Wisdom coexists with prudence. Wisdom possesses knowledge, and discretion. Earlier recall that we had a discussion of the knowledge of God, that in some sense is considered beyond wisdom. Now we have a paradoxical situation where wisdom is at the Apex of these character traits. Wisdom has counsel, sound, judgment, and insight. This we are told is power.

The importance of wisdom is emphasized, starting in verse 15 for the political reign and governance of the people. This includes kings and rulers and princes and nobles. We are told that anyone who seeks wisdom will find wisdom. There is some universality in that rulers everywhere may achieve wisdom. We also read that wisdom loves those who love her. In this sense we may have a different perspective than for example the phrase for God, so loved the world.... There we see that God first loves with an opportunity for us to reciprocate. Here, in the case of wisdom, we are rewarded with more wisdom, simply by trying to revere it in the first place.

In verse 21 we are told that there is a rich inheritance for those who love wisdom. This is not just an intellectual or spiritual inheritance, but rather an actual physical prosperity. Now we come once again to the creation of wisdom, in which wisdom was the first creation by the Lord God. indeed, wisdom goes on to give measures of creation that came after her, whether it is the water or mountains or earth. Wisdom was created even before the heavens were set in place. Not only that but wisdom was the constant companion of the Lord God.

Altar goes so far as to note that conceivably this wisdom is the inspiration behind the opening chapter of the gospel of John. Then we were told that in the beginning was the Word and the Word was with God and the Word was God. Certainly, it does not take much extrapolation to say that the wisdom that we are describing here fits this concept. Alter also points out that verse 30 is meant to be a depiction of wisdom as the delightful companion of God. He also notes that there is a playfulness character to this description. The chapter closes with a blessing for those who listen to wisdom, and a curse to those who do not.

Proverbs – Chapter 9

Chapter 9 concludes a section that Fox maintains is an entirely different style and therefore different author than the rest of Proverbs. Other scholars like Alter have come to agree with his persuasive arguments. This is the conclusion therefore of the Lady Wisdom section. This chapter is also both a symmetrical chapter, a metaphorical chapter, and comparison and contrast chapter. The main players are Lady Wisdom, of course, along with the seductress.

Like Genesis this chapter begins with creating or building something. She employs the number 7 for historical and religious significance. There is a table prepared that exceeds that of David in the twenty third Psalm. David has a nondescript table. Maybe the cup is there for David, but Lady Wisdom has meat and wine and a special setting. Once again we see that she has the vantage point of height. She uses that vantage point to call out to others to join in. She has a cadre of young women maids in her service to do so.

Yet after we are given the impression that the young women will be her voice, we see Lady Wisdom using her own voice. Her message is universal. It is for the simple minded and the wise alike. Yet realistically she knows that most simple minded people as well as those who make fun of others simply will reject her message. This is in contrast to a wise person who will deepen their wisdom further by lis more. We see echoes of this in the New Testament where we read that to whomever much is given that much is required. Fox presents compelling evidence that verses 7-10 were interjected by another author.

An eternal platitude begins the second half of the chapter where we are told that the fear of the Lord is the beginning of wisdom. The second part of that verse adds that knowledge of the Holy One is understanding. So, we have this inescapable bond between knowledge and wisdom that is prevalent throughout the first 9 chapters. It is not a fear of punishment from God but a respect for wisdom that is being conveyed. Then we are told basically that you will reap what you sow.

In verse12 we note that those who are wise will be rewarded in their wisdom. Yet mockers suffer alone as nature would have a mocker to do. Then we transition to Lady Folly who is also the equivalent of the seductress. She appeals to the simple minded and those who lack judgment. Her words are exactly the same in verse 16 that Lady Wisdom utters in verse 4. Yet the intention is exactly the opposite as becomes clear in the concluding verses. There we see that the powers of deception are a gateway to the grave.

Proverbs – Chapter 10

Proverbs chapter 10 begins a whole other section in style and likely different author than chapters 1 through nine. Alter points out that the head note or title does not necessarily mean claim for authorship for king Solomon. Rather it may be just referencing that it is in the style of Solomon. There is not a storyline or continuous poem like occurs in many of the chapters 1 through nine. Rather, this is a random collection of miscellaneous one line Proverbs. There are often contrasts in the sayings where distinctions are made from righteous to wicked, etc. within a couplet or verse.

Indeed, the opening verse notes that a wise son brings joy to his father but a foolish son brings grief to his mother. This is almost a double contrast with wise and foolish and father and mother. The notion that the mother would bear the brunt of grief while the father took the delightful portion may be something still carried over from this ancient saying for better or worse. Being righteous delivers someone from death we are told in verse 2 in contrast to ill-gotten treasures.

Verse 3 contrasts the righteous who will not go hungry unlike the craving of the wicked. We see an amplification of this in the sermon on the mount where Jesus basically gives only the upside of the couplet and notes that blessed are those who hunger and thirst for righteousness for, they will be satisfied. Laziness is vilified next while diligence is rewarded. This is a recurring theme throughout Proverbs. The closest thing to this in the Beatitudes would be the meek who inherit the earth. The righteous have a memory for posterity while the wicked do not.

We come to an interesting notion in verse 10 where we read about a malicious wink causing grief. Fox notes that this is an expression of hostility. Indeed we have mention of violence in verse 11 and hatred in verse 12. In verse 13 we have a little run on wisdom. Wisdom is found on those who discern. They not only receive the material rewards mentioned earlier but they also store up wisdom itself. Again the New Testament equivalent may be to he who is given talents will be given more. Fox points out that in some settings in Proverbs that the term lazy is better served by timidity or lawlessness. So too is sluggard sometimes better represented by impious.

By verse 16, we read that the effort to be righteous is a lifelong pursuit. This does require to be clear, some reproof as opposed to those who forsake rebuke, and are led astray. Of course, anyone who slanders is a fool, but this might come simply from someone talking too much. Meanwhile, the words from a righteous man guide many people. The author knows that doing foul ball measures is like a sport for the fool. By the same token, so is wisdom for the person of wisdom and discernment.

In the storm of life, the wicked will perish with the righteous last because they fear the Lord who will lengthen their days. Even the longing of the righteous is a joy. When we compare Proverbs, with another wisdom book of Job, we note that adversity does get to Job, but the Proverbs tell us adversity will sweep away the wicked. Altar goes on to note that verse 32 has an antithetical parallelism to it, which involves not only acting or speaking in a contorted way but even in disconcerting others through such behavior. This contrasts with the righteous man whose speech has the capacity to please others, and win their goodwill.

Proverbs – Chapter 11

Proverbs chapter 11, begins with a challenge to be honest in the commercial world. We naturally might try to read into this as applying to some type of social justice. The reality is that this was meant only for a business process with the emphasis of being fair. Certainly, that is applicable today. Then we have an abrupt transition to discussing pride and the disgrace that comes with that as opposed to humility. This is followed by comparing integrity and unfaithful. As Fox points out their is a type of vindictive joy when the wicked suffer.

We are told him first for that wealth is worthless in the day of wrath, but that righteousness will deliver from death. this theme is repeated serval different ways in the following verses. Fox notes the technique where a translator has introduced an allusion to the afterlife in verse 7. To be sure though many translators do not perceive a true reference to the afterlife in Proverbs. The prosperity gospel can point to verse 10 where we are told that when the righteous prosper, the city rejoices. Alter points out that the storyline in verse eight is comical, because it suggests that the righteous man is extricated from a tight spot in which he was physically jammed, while the wicked is immediately popped into that spot.

Much of the rest of the chapter is full of aphorisms. We are told that gossip betrays confidence. We are told that many advisers make victory sure for a nation as opposed to a lack of guidance. We have the practical advice of being cautious about putting up security for another person. In a culture that valued men and money, we are told that a kind hearted woman gains respect, but that ruthless men gain only wealth.

In verse 18 we have a version of reaping what you sow. The wicked man after all earns deceptive wages, but the righteous will sow righteousness, and reap their reward, which we are told later is life. Sometimes we are given riddles in the first half of the verse such as in verse 22. The set up is the comparison of a gold ring in a pig's snout. The answer to this is a beautiful woman who shows no discretion.

In verse 24 we have an early version of what is known as the Matthew effect. We are told one man gives freely yet gains even more. On the other hand, the person who withholds unduly comes to poverty. This is, indeed the principle, behind the parable of the talents in the New Testament, as told by Matthew. The last verse of his chapter notes that if the righteous receive their due on earth, then how much more the ungodly and sinner.

In the New Testament, we are warned about storing up for the future for ourselves. This is the story of the rich man who stored up grain for himself, and suggested that all he needed to do at that point was to eat drink, and be merry. We have that precaution in verse 26 where we are told, that people curse the man who hordes grain. For the individual who does not have the New Testament understanding of future reward it becomes essential to have both the reward and punishment now as Proverbs tends to promote.

Proverbs – Chapter 12

Proverbs chapter 12 starts out with comparison and contrast of those who love the Lord and discipline and knowledge. They are blessed compared to the condemnation for the opposite. Next, we have the comparison of a good wife with a disgraceful wife. It has been noted that the noble character wife is a crown, but the disgraceful wife is a decay in her husband's bones, which deleterious impact might be greater than the benefit from the crown.

Next, it is time for more comparisons and opposites in which the righteous are just, and their upright speech rescues them. In addition, they stand firm in their house. Of course, the opposite applies to the wicked. Meanwhile, a righteous man cares for even his animals' basic needs while the wicked have only cruelty. The positive work ethic is also celebrated in verse 11. The righteous will escape trouble and the root of the righteous will flourish.

Next, we are told that a wise man listens to advice compared to the fool whose ways always seem right to himself. A fool is also easily annoyed, compared to a prudent man who overlooks insults. Reckless words are piercing compared to the healing of the wise persons tongue. The truth is eternal on the righteous lips. Peacemakers will obtain joy according this chapter in Proverbs. This is not greatly different than the sermon on the mount, and which peace-makers will be called sons of God.

Profound and simple statements are found in abundance in Proverbs. The notion that a prudent person keeps his knowledge to himself, while the heart of fools blurts out folly is an eternal truth. after some more admonition for the western work ethic, we were told about the dangers of an anxious heart compared to a kind word. Other random versus close this out by noting that a righteous man is cautious in friendship, compared to the way of the wicked, who are led astray.

Proverbs – Chapter 13

In the opening verse, we were told that a wise son, heeds his father's instruction. Altar explains that the original Hebrew is much more economical. It uses merely four words, without any verb wise/son/fathers/reproof. The brevity and economy is illuminating. The second verse compares the difference between the healthy fruit of the righteous coming from the lips compared to the craving for violence. If we were to substitute appetite for violence, we would then realize how much stronger the meaning of craving here.

In verse three we are told that the prudent man keeps his mouth shut as a prerequisite to guarding his soul. The theme of cravings continues by noting that those who are lazy crave, but get nothing. The diligent worker, however, is fully satisfied. verse seven warns us that it is one thing to appear rich, but not have true wealth by which is meant principles and all of the concepts that precede this. Meanwhile, others may appear poor on the outside, but have great riches internally in their soul.

On the surface verse eight tends to suggest the benefit of material possessions in that the rich may have a security for ransom. We believe, though the depth of this proverb is explained by what is normally the -2nd half of a proverb. Here we are told that the poor man does not hear a threat. On the surface this means that they have no material possessions to lose and therefore do not perceive any threat. However, this may be a premonition or foreshadowing of the New Testament statement by Jesus of not storing up treasures on earth.

We return to more practical economical advice in verse 11. There we are told that dishonest money will wither away. However, those who gather little by little are able to make it grow. Perhaps this is a can of foreshadowing of the parable of the talents in the New Testament. Furthermore, it is, perhaps a warning for speculative investment. Indeed we are told in the next verse that the alternate route board for a worse person is the fountain of life.

Verse 19 is a challenging verse in which we were told that a longing that is fulfilled is sweet to the soul. Alter explains the connection with the word throat, but that there is an alternative explanation that could mean it is to the essential being. A short while later we were told that misfortune pursues the sinner. This seeming inversion of the order of how this happens is a great insight. We are told that a poor man's field might produce abundant yield, but that injustice would sweep it away. This verse is indeed hard to reconcile with the rest of the chapter, and arguably all of Proverbs. Indeed, Alter believes this verse to be more fitting to the book of Ecclesiastes, in which absurdities that cannot be explained in this world, tend to abound.

Proverbs – Chapter 14

Proverbs chapter 14 opens with a verse that is similar to chapter 9 the first verse. Since the historical case is made, that chapter 9 was written after chapter 14 we might surmise that this is the original. Indeed, since the theme of the first nine chapters is Lady Wisdom, we can see how the wise woman was ultimately translated into Lady Wisdom. In verse three, we have the contrast between the arrogant speech of the fool versus the prudent speech of the righteous.

In the fourth verse, we have a moment of reflection. In this situation, where there are no actions in the manger, it is empty and clean. However, it is the situation with all of its actions including dirt and excrement that allows an animal to contribute to the abundant harvest. The next verse is somewhat of a tautology, where a true witness does not deceive, and a false witness pours out lies. This is after all the definition of a false witness.

Verse eight when read carefully, tells us that not only are fools deceptive, but that they also deceive themselves. The author is not keen on people who mock others. He knows they may seek wisdom as noted in verse six, but not find it. However, their biggest mistake is scoffing at the idea of making amends for one's sins. This way may seem right initially, but it is a pathway to death we are told in verse 12. They are partners with the faithless who will be repaid for their ways.

Amidst all of these platitudes, we have the aphorism in which the heart knows its own bitterness. A few verses later, we see that even in the laughter, the heart may ache, and the joy may end in grief. verse 14 does not have the usual language of the extreme differences between the wise person, and the fool. Rather both are rewarded for their actions. This is the concept of reap what you sow. That wise person fears the Lord, while the fool remains reckless and hot headed.

Verse 20 seems a bit out of place for Proverbs when we were told that the poor are shunned even by their neighbors while the rich have many friends. This does not seem to be a statement of fairness. However, right after this, we are told that he who despises his neighbor, commits a sin, and he who is kind to the needy, which would include the neighbor, is blessed. The point here is that it is difficult to reconcile this degree of contradiction.

A few verses later, we see that the hard work ethic is extolled, as is a truthful witness, and those who fear the Lord, which is also a fountain of life. Patience carries the reward of understanding. Perhaps it contributes to the next verse number 30 in which we are told a heart at peace gives life to the body. This is compared to the corrosion in the contrasting portion of the verse. to be clear, there is one final statement in which we are told that whoever is kind to the needy, honors God.

Proverbs – Chapter 15

This chapter begins with a familiar platitude in that a gentle answer turns away wrath, whereas a harsh word stirs up anger. After another familiar presentation of the difference between the wise and the foolish, we have a more universal statement. In verse three, we read that the eyes of the Lord are everywhere, including the wicked, as well as the good. We see echoes of this in the New Testament in the sermon on the mount in which Jesus notes that God makes his rain fall on the just and the unjust.

Verse five shows the value of discipline, which, of course is spurned by the foolish. Treasure awaits the righteous. To be clear this is meant in the material sense and not the spiritual in this context. In the material sense though we say that God cannot be bought by sacrifice, because the sacrifice of the wicked is detested by God. Leaving the path of righteousness leads to stern discipline, and possibly even death. This could include even those who scoff at correction. Alter points out that in verse 11 the Hebrew words are synonyms, in which, even the depths of perdition are supposed with transparency for God's scrutiny.

Next, we enter some measures of the heart in which we are told that a happy heart makes the face cheerful as opposed to the heart ache which crushes the spirit. According to Alter this good heartedness does not mean kindness or benevolence, but instead a good mood. Meanwhile the heart which discerns is constantly seeking knowledge, as opposed to the fool whose mouth feeds on folly. It is better to have the fear of the Lord in the heart than to have great wealth which promotes turmoil.

In verse 20 we see a repetition of the distinction that the joy which comes to the father, from a wise son, as opposed to the foolish man, who despises his mother. Even in a patriarchal culture, the recognition of both parent's benefit is very evident. This sentiment is captured in the sixth commandment which instructs us to honor our parents, so that our days on the earth may be long. We might suggest that the next verse is meant to occur in juxtaposition, in that one who lacks judgment from their parents will instead delight in folly.

Verse 22 offers another familiar platitude about failing to plan, which is essentially planning to fail. We have seen this same concept in earlier Proverbs. Closely paired with this is the benefit of a timely word. Shortly thereafter we are told that the Lord knows the thoughts of the pure. Indeed, the echo of this statement occurs in Matthew chapter 5 in the beatitudes in which we are told blessed are the pure in heart, for they will see God. Another beatitude predecessor occurs in verse 29 where God hears the prayers of the righteous. In the beatitudes, we are told that blessed are the people who hunger and thirst for righteousness, for they will be filled. The chapter closes with an admonition for humility, which is more important than honor.

Proverbs – Chapter 16

The first verse of Proverbs chapter 16 opens with a little bit different verse combination than most other Proverbs. Indeed, one needs to think a little bit deeper here. To men belong the plans of the heart. Here we might think mind, or at least inner soul. However, the second part of this is, but from the Lord comes the reply of the tongue. Does this mean from God himself or that God gives us the words to say as human beings that is separate from the planned-out machinations of humans?

God, indeed, looks in to the motives of a persons, heart, and ways, and on them, even when those actions seem innocent to the individual. God has a time for everything, including the wicked, who have a day of disaster coming. This chapter also has the concept of atonement through love and faithfulness as we note in verse six. When a person's actions are pleasing to the lord, even his enemies live at peace with him. The notion that the lips of a king speak as an oracle in verse 10 is contradicted in the book of Ecclesiastes.

142

A king, like God will become angry and full of wrath. A wise man is able to appease this anger. By verse 18, we have another platitude in which we note that pride goes before a fall. indeed, it is common for that way to appear right to a person as we note in verse 25 and still have that pathway lead to death. In verse 26 we see the benefit of an appetite driving the laborer's ability to work. This is no less the case with someone who hunger and thirst for righteousness, as we read about in the beatitudes in Matthew chapter 5. Patience is rewarded.

Proverbs – Chapter 17

Chapter 17 opens with a couplet that appears to be rather obvious. However, we must recognize that the focus on peace and quiet overcomes a connection with sacrifice. Indeed, we are told in the footnotes, as well as by Alter that the feasting is in reference to the leftover food after a sacrifice. The strife therefore, is not merely from household strife, but may reference the strife that goes on in one's own heart and mind when they feel they have earned something such as a feast by giving something such as a sacrifice.

Next, we are told that inheritance by mere heredity is not as important as wisdom, and in the lowliest of servants. Meanwhile, God does not care so much about gold and silver, but rather the heart. In verse five we see that those who mock the poor have contempt for their Maker. Grandparents are pleased to see verse six, in which grandchildren are noted to be a crown to the aged. The couplet of that verse does not have the usual contrast, but rather shows that parents may likewise be the pride of their children in a paradoxical fashion.

Despite the admonition against bribery elsewhere, we are told in verse eight that the bribe is a charm to the one who gives it. This foreshadows the New Testament parable, in which the steward of the land, forgave debts and settled of accounts, which turned out to be beneficial. Fox notes that one interpretation of verse 8 is that instruction is a reward of grace when used appropriately. Certainly, this is a classic situation of the benefit of exegesis. The next verse adds to that in which someone who overcomes an offense, promotes love as opposed to the person who repeats the matter which leads to separation of friendship.

The forerunner of turning the other cheek is noted in verse 13 in which we are told, if a man pays back evil for good, then evil will never leave his house. Jesus takes us a step further by noting that even paying back evil for evil has is own downside. Continuing, we note that dropping a quarrel is important before a dispute breaks out. This is again a foreshadowing of Jesus statement to make friends quickly with your accuser while you are on the way to court.

A true friend will love us at all times. The second part of this couplet notes that a brother is born for adversity. This does not necessarily need to be a negative portion of the couplet, even though we are conditioned for that set up. Indeed, to love a quarrel is to love sin. There is no better medicine than a cheerful heart, which is contrasted with a crushed spirit which dries up the bones. This chapter closes with the value of restraining temper and restraining words. After all, even a fool, may look wise if he holds his tongue.

Proverbs – Chapter 18

The first verse of chapter 18 associate's selfishness with being unfriendly. This also defies sound judgment. Close to this is the fool who delights in airing or expressing his own opinions. Following this, we have a number of common-sense utterances. In verse 10, we have the poetic notion that the name of the Lord is a strong tower, the righteous run into it and are safe. Indeed, this verse has been incorporated into a song. We then have a familiar platitude in verse 12, in which receive pride comes before a fall.

We have an eternal truth in verse 13 reminding us to listen before we answer. Following this, we are reminded that a person's spirit sustains them in sickness. Medically speaking, this is still quite true today. Verse 16 is a standalone without a couplet of opposites. There we are told that the gift opens the way for the giver, and ushers him into the presence of the great. In verse 22 Fox gives a variant reading that if you get rid of a good wife, that you are getting rid of happiness. This happiness is contrasted with the temporary pleasure of the adulteress. The last verse points out that having lots of companions is not nearly as important as the friend who is closer than a brother.

Proverbs – Chapter 19

The first verse opens with the notion of walking the straight and narrow, which is better than a fool who uses twisted speech. Next, we see the folly of having energy and passion, but without knowledge. The next statement in verse four is a puzzle about wealth bringing friends, but a poor man has his friends desert him. Alter has suggested that this is not so much wisdom as merely a practical observation. Later, we see the extension that a poor man is even shunned by his relatives, and yet more so his friends.

We are told twice in the same chapter a few verses apart in verse five, and in verse nine that a false witness will not go unpunished. The second part of the couplet is only slightly changed with the first time being that he will not go free and the second ending is that he will perish. While those two themes are related there is certainly potentially a long ways in between them in terms of severity. It is of course, wisdom, which gives a person patience.

We have some of the usual standard scenes about a foolish son, or a quarrelsome wife, but we see the blessings of prudent work, which is from the Lord. We see once again, the folly of laziness. then we come to a paradoxical statement about he who is kind to the poor lends to the Lord. Perhaps, after we have removed the laziness and recognize that it is not someone's fault if they are not lazy if they are poor, and their friends and family ignore them. we are told such a person gains a reward. This is carried out to a further extreme in Matthew chapter 26 with the sheep and goats: I was hungry and you fed me, etc.

Discipline is again extolled, but so is avoiding violence to the point of death. There is a warning about rescuing a hot tempered person, because such an act will have to be repeated. listening to advice and accepting instruction is a pathway to the wise. Then we come to another gem in which we are told that what a man desires is unfailing love. With this, we have the fear of the Lord leading to life. Towards the conclusion of this chapter, we see some indirect recommendation to honor your parents.

Proverbs – Chapter 20

The first verse of chapter 20 seems to be a warning against alcohol. Alter points out, though that the reference is to strong drink made from grapes and not simply alcohol in general. One can easily see the connection with verse three in which it is noted that it is a men's honor to avoid strife and like the fool who is quick to quarrel. This is, of course, the outcome of too much or too strong of alcohol. Verse five is an interesting statement, in that we are told that the purpose of a man's heart is from deep waters, but that a man of understanding can draw them out.

Verse nine offers the rhetorical question of who can say I have kept my heart pure and I am clean without sin? Here we see some resemblance in the story of John chapter 8 with the prostitute who is caught in the act and brought to Jesus who challenges leaders to throw the first stone, whoever among them is without sin. We also see echoes of this in the rich young ruler, who presents to Jesus, looking for eternal life, and claims to have kept all of the Commandments which proposition remains unchallenged by Jesus.

The 14th verse gives us a challenge. Experts of the hidden Hebrew language note that a very plausible situation is one in which the reading is that the product is cheap and or denigrated in some way shape or form, and then when the price is reduced, the purchase is made. Even then gold and rubies may be an abundance, but they are much rarer than lips which speak knowledge. That knowledge may be simply getting the proper advice if you should happen to find yourself at war.

Verse 21 gives a warning about an inheritance that comes quickly at the beginning. This will not likely be blessed or stick around to the end. Immediately following this is the injunction to avoid paying someone back for a wrong. Rather the second half of the couplet reminds us that if we wait on the Lord, we will be delivered. Even something dedicated to the Lord rashly they turn out to have significant problems. We recall the story in the Original Testament in which someone promised their daughter for a certain outcome that came about.

Proverbs – Chapter 21

In the first verse of chapter 21 we return to the theme of the deep waters of the heart. In verse five of chapter 20 we were told that the purpose of a man's heart is deep waters. This time the king has taken over the heart. He put it in the hand of the Lord, like a one hour course which he directs according to his pleasure. The Lord will weigh the ways of a man's heart, not the thoughts of a person who thinks that they are right. actually, doing what is right though, and just is more important than any sacrifice that can be made.

After this strong opening of some deeper thinking, we have a return to the usual precaution about haughty eyes, and a proud heart. We have the reward of being diligent as deposed to ill-gotten gains through deceit and violence. Then we have a random verse that notes it is better to have a difficult place to get to and live in than to have all the space in the world and live with constant dissent with a partner. Alter points out the riddle contained in this verse.

We have another complex riddle in verse 11. We might ask which is better: knowledge or wisdom? We might ask which is a preferred way to learn: through punishment or through instruction. As obvious as this might be to us the verse tells us that when the mocker is punished that he gets wisdom but that the wise man gets knowledge through instruction. Granted the intention here is to show that the wise benefit from listening to instruction whereas those less inclined need to have some other methods to drill it into them.

Proverbs is a mixed bag when it comes to the poor. That is unless you realize that we have 2 types of poor. First is those who are poor because of their lack of diligence. The other type is those who simply have misfortune or poor inheritance. Verse 13 appears to refer to the latter. There we are told that the cries of those who ignore the poor will go unheeded. The next verse when split is perhaps meant to be a corollary in which a gift given in secret can soothe anger including the anger of being poor through no fault of one's own.

Justice remains a source of joy for the righteous, but of course it is terror to evil doers. He who loves pleasure will become poor. This is followed about precaution with wine and oil. We must be careful here with the application of anachronistic standard. In fact, a few verses later, we are told that in the house of the wise are stores of choice, food and oil

Once again, we have a warning about being better to live in a desert than with a quarrelsome or ill-tempered wife. When this is paired with verse nine, we have only a slightly different version. If indeed we consider chapters 10 through 31 haven't been written historically before chapters 1 through nine, we see that perhaps the personification of the loose woman in chapters 1 through nine is the amalgamation of all of these more extant people.

We are told that the lazy person has a craving that cannot be satisfied. Yet their sacrifice is detestable, because they are not sincere in their hearts. The righteous on the other hand, give without sparing anything. This is not to say that the upright gives no thought to their ways we were told a few versus later. They calculate they are giving of both time and material possessions. When it is all said, and done though, verse 30 puts a nice summary in that there is no wisdom or insight, or plan that can succeed against the Lord.

Proverbs – Chapter 22

This chapter opens with a simple platitude about a good name being better than great riches. To further add to the relative notion of material possessions in the second verse notes that the Lord God made both rich and poor. Humility and honor are extolled. Verse six has another eternal platitude. There we were told to train a child in the way that he should go, and when he is old, he will not turn from it. Many have learned the King James Version of this, and as Alter notes, we really cannot improve upon it.

Next we have some more sayings that basically comes down to reaping what you sow. There is a recognition of sharing with the poor. Again, in verse 16 we are warned not to oppress the poor merely to increase one's own wealth. Continuing to reach out and care for the poor theme in verse 22 where we are instructed to avoid exploiting the poor because they are poor. We are told that God will exact vengeance on such an individual. This plays off of the theme in verse nine in which the generous people are blessed when they share their food with the poor. Fox notes that one of the possible interpretations of these verses is the eschatological perspective that ultimately the poor will rule over the rich.

We are given a warning to not hang out with people who are angered easily or hot tempered, because these ways rub off on ourselves. Verse 10 suggest that we get rid of a pest or the bad apple, so it does not spoil the whole assembly. There is some more practical advice about caution of putting up security for someone else's debts because we our-selves may lose even the bed that we sleep on. Finally, we are given an expectation to develop our talent or skill, much like the parable of the talents in the New Testament. When we do so, we will have our rightful place among kings and will not be relegated to obscurity.

Proverbs – Chapter 23

There is a fair amount of information given in the first several verses of this chapter. We are instructed to observe carefully what is before us, when we sit down to dine with a ruler. There is a precaution that if we are given to gluttony that we would be better off to put a knife to our throat. Jesus gives a similar admonition in the New Testament. There is no instruction not to eat with the ruler. There is even some suggestion that either the ruler has conditioned himself to either handle the delicacies before him, or to avoid them. There is the suggestion that it is a matter of quantity that allows one to avoid gluttony. We are not told to avoid the delicacies, but rather to not crave them because such food is deceptive.

This concept of avoiding the pitfalls of richness continues in verse four where we are told to not over strive and wear ourselves out by seeking to get rich. We are cautioned to have restraint through wisdom. Again, we were not told to avoid material possessions, but rather the stress of seeking them. This is followed by the statement that when we cast of glance at riches, they will be gone as though they have sprouted wings and flown off like an eagle.

Verse four contains a mixture of possible meanings when we are told to avoid the food of a stingy man. We are told not to crave his delicacies. Is the discussion here because the stingy person eats only fit food for someone else? Is it because when we crave the delicacies such that we will become like him and be stingy. Is it the craving itself in general that is the problem? After all, such an individual may be telling us to eat and drink, but his heart is not into the communion.

We are given some precautions to avoid changing things that are set in stone. By the same token, we are precautioned to not take what belongs to the fatherless who otherwise may have no resources. However, as Alter notes, their redeemer is strong. We also might consider this a reference to God. Alter notes that it might also refer to a human redeemer. Altar also notes the connection with the judicial term as is used in the book of Job, and in the book of Ruth.

In verse 13 there is a sudden change to the repetition of earlier admonitions about the benefit of discipline and the consequences when it is not applied. There is warning to not envy sinners. After all, there is hope for a better future that does not have to involve that envy. There is precaution of the dangers of strong wine. This is followed by admonitions to honor your parents throughout their life. This is naturally tied with obtaining wisdom and discipline and understanding. This brings great joy to the parents. The chapter closes with a series of verses showing the consequences of excess alcohol tied in with the dangers of prostitution.

Proverbs – Chapter 24

This chapter begins with some rather simplistic considerations of not desiring to be in the company of wicked men, or to envy them in any way, because their hearts promote violence. Instead, we are to build our homes with wisdom and fill the rooms with knowledge. These are rare and beautiful treasures. They also instill power in people. That wise individual has great strength through knowledge. The wise person is good counsel when it comes time to wage war. To be clear this is the old fashion physical combat and not the emotional or spiritual war.

There is a warning for those who plot schemes. We are told that if we fall during times of trouble, then our strength is small. This does not say it will not happen, but rather it appears as a challenge to increase our overall strength. We are challenged to provide a rescue to those who are being led to death. The term slaughter is used here as though to compare such a death with animals. We cannot claim innocence through lack of knowledge, because we are to use our hearts to perceive and discern needs. Indeed, this type of warning would serve well, for those who claimed they knew nothing about persecution in World War two.

In verse 13 we see the recommendation to eat honey because it is good and is sweet. When this is connected with the next verse of wisdom, we recognize it as a purposeful pairing of concepts that wisdom is meant to be sweet. In verse 16 we are once again told that a righteous person will indeed fall down. However, the application here is after falling 7 times, all seven times he rose again, as opposed to wicked person who may be brought down by a simple fall. This number is meant to be symbolic of unlimited strength as opposed to a particular numerical limitation.

By the same token, although the enemy or wicked may fall and stumble, we are told not to rejoice over this phenomenon, because God sees this and disapproves. This is again appears to be a foreshadowing of New Testament theology, where we are instructed, to pray for our enemies. We are not to fret about such evil people, because they really do not have a future, and they will be snuffed out. Rather, we are to fear both the Lord and the king.

Proverbs – Chapter 25

There is a special heading as though to indicate both the connection with Solomon and a new segment. Playing off the theme of kingship is that it is the glory of kings to search out a matter whereas it is the glory of God to conceal a matter. This pattern is seen several times in this collection, in which there is a potent image in the first portion of the couplet, followed by its earthly antithesis. Keeping with the theme of kings, we are told that it is better to not claim honor in front of a nobleman lest you be humiliated.

Next, we have some practical advice of not going quickly to court, just because we may have seen something by our neighbor. If, after all our neighbor may put us to shame, if we don't understand the circumstances. Perhaps we think we saw something that we did not see or did not have enough details. Under such cases, your neighbor, may sue you and you may lose your reputation. On the other hand, an appropriately timed statement is like silver and gold. The earthly analogy is that it is a wise man's rebuke to those who will listen.

When we find something that appears sweet, we are not cautioned to avoid it, but to not have too much of it. So doing causes us to vomit just as our neighbor might feel if we are in their home too much. Along the theme of neighbors is the very important precept to not give false witness against our neighbor. Whereas one could argue that this is covered in the original 10 Commandments, this is a more practical notation. By the same token, singing songs to a heavy heart is like rubbing salt in the wound.

Next, we have some expression of universality by reaching out to our enemy, if they are hungry or thirsty. This foreshadows, the New Testament story of the sheep and goats found in Matthew chapter 25: I was hungry and you fed me. I was thirsty, and you gave me a drink. We were told here that in so doing we are heaping burning coals on our enemies head. We return to the concept of a happy home as opposed to that which has a quarrelsome wife, in which case it would be better to live on the corner of the roof. The chapter closes once again with the self-control theme once again, detected with the precaution of not eating too much honey.

Proverbs – Chapter 26

This chapter is a hodgepodge of collective seems almost as if it was left over sayings that needed to be included somewhere. There are even contradictory elements within this chapter. There are many riddles or puzzles that are presented in paradoxical fashion. for example, at the start, we're told that honor does not fit a fool just as snow does not fit summer time. In verse number two we are told that an undeserved curse is like winged creatures that fly away. Of note, there is not an admonition to not curse.

Verses four and five appear to be opposite recommendations in which we are told it is best to not answer a fool according to his folly lest we become like him. Immediately after that, we are told to answer a full according to his folly, or he will thank he is wise. On one level, this back-to-back contradiction may simply have been an editorial error. On the other hand, we might construe that the solution lies in presenting the answer on one's own terms, as opposed to the terms of the foolish.

Verse number six becomes graphic with its incorporation of violence. When we rely on messages or knowledge to be transmitted by fools, it is like cutting off your own feet or drinking violence. Such a message is like the lame man's legs which are limp. After we are given several more comparisons, we have the very descriptive notion of the fool who repeats his folly, been likened to a dog returning to his vomit.

Despite these permanent descriptions of the fool, there is something worse. That is the notion of being wise in your own eyes. Within transition to the notion that a sluggard or lazy individual is also wise in his own eyes. The couplets here tell us otherwise. Getting into someone else's quarrel is like trying to grab a ravenous dog. Alter points out the significance of this in that dog at that time were not domesticated in ancient Israel, making them more fierce in all likelihood.

The chapter closes with another series of unconnected sayings. We are told that her quarrel will die out without gossip, just as a fire goes out without wood. Meanwhile those words of a gossip, are like choice food that get lodged in a person's inmost body. We are precautioned about the speech of someone malicious. It is somewhat like a person, who digs a pit, then, falls into it themselves. After all a lying tongue hates those it hurts just as flattery can ruin someone.

Proverbs – Chapter 27

The opening verse of this chapter calls to mind something from the New Testament in the sermon on the mount. In this particular verse, we read to not boast about tomorrow, for we do not know what a day may bring forth. This contrasts with the sermon on the mount, where we are told not to worry about tomorrow, but to let the days own trouble be sufficient. Both of these verses suggest that there will be troubles in our lives with the Original Testament focusing on not boasting about what is to come, whereas the New Testament focuses on the Now moment of today

After the essential statement to not toot your own horn, we are given several riddles. The first one is what would be heavy like a stone, and a burden like sand. That answer is a fool who is heavier than both. The next riddle would be what is worse than anger, which is cruel, and fury, which is overwhelming. That answer would be jealousy. Next we have a comparison of the wounds of a friend, such as some word that might be said on our behalf, and yet hurts us in some way is better than the profuse kisses from the enemy.

We are told that there comes a time when we can have too much of a good thing, such as honey when we are full. On the other hand, when we are hungry, almost anything can taste sweet. In the New Testament, we get an upgrade in that those who hunger and thirst for righteousness will be satisfied. The value of friendship is extolled, especially in the face of calamity, in which the hospitality of that friend would be greater than even that of a brother. Indeed, a good neighbor nearby is better than a brother far away.

Of course, the so-called good neighbor thing can go too far if for example, our neighbor is loudly blessing us early in the morning, which may be a little bit over the top. The chapter continues with some verses that are near duplicates of earlier Proverbs. For example, we have the reference again to the quarrelsome wife. It is indeed impossible to hide her because she is everywhere. By tending to a fig tree, we will literally reap the fruits of our rewards.

There are some profound statements made such as first 19, in which we are told that as water reflects a face so a man's heart reflects the man. Finally, just as the eyes of man are never satisfied so too are death and destruction not satisfied ever. The message here is a strong precaution about lusting with the eyes which is then in turn taken to heart and then precedes to death and destruction. Man is tested by the praise that he receives. Finally, we are told to know well the condition of our own flocks, because they provide for us some basics of life. The practicality of this was noted by the ancients and again capitalized by Jesus in the New Testament.

Proverbs – Chapter 28

Alter explains the first verse as meaning that when the wicked flee without anyone pursuing them, it is because their conscience is getting to them unlike the righteous who have confidence of doing the right thing. The multiple of this is when an entire country is in rebellion, there will be many rulers who are trying to gain power. However, order comes about simply by people of understanding. Such people do not oppress the poor, which is like a driving rain leaving no crops.

However, it is better to be a poor man with a blameless walk, then a rich person whose ways are perverse. People who seek justice will understand that they need to serve the poor. Again, we are reminded to avoid increasing wealth by excess interest which is in turn unkind to the poor. continuing with the theme of rich versus poor, we see in verse

11, that, although a rich man is wise in his own eyes, it is a poor man with discernment who sees through him.

In verse 13 we read that a person who conceals sins does not prosper, but that whoever confesses and renounces them finds mercy. when we recognize the next verse as blessing a person who always fears the Lord, we see that confession is compatible with fear and respect to the Lord God. Fox notes that in verse 21 that where we read that a man will do wrong for a piece of bread uses the same language as when Joseph was sold into slavery by his brothers. We then have the usual precautions about flattery and greed, as well as the admonition to respect one's parents. The conclusion of this chapter once again uplift the responsibility of caring for the poor.

Proverbs – Chapter 29

This chapter opens with the negative consequences of not attending to proper reviews from other people. The chapter then delves into platitudes, and a repeat of many of the same themes that we have discussed earlier. It is justice that gives a country stability, but greed that tears it down. Furthermore, righteous people care about justice for the poor. Furthermore, the wise person knows how to deflect anger. This type of integrity bothers wicked people.

While it is hard to beat chapter 28 for concern about the poor, there are still some additional measures to be said for them. The Lord gives sight and insight to the poor person we are told in verse 13. In addition, if a king judges' rapport with fairness, then such a throne will always be secure. Indirectly this always, or forever clause ties into what king David himself sought, but was often insecure with. Peace in the kingdom begins with peace on the home front, which intern begins with discipline. The rest of the chapter deals with precaution about speaking in haste, or pampering, a servant and the dangers of being hot tempered or having too much pride. Through all of this, it is only God who gives justice.

Proverbs – Chapter 30

According to both Fox and Alter, the first portion of chapter 30 has an entirely different background and authorship from the rest of the book. There is a brief biography of the supposed author, which lasts about four verses. The end of this section likely ends with verse nine. This book provides fundamentals with some meat for their purpose of scripture. We are told in verse five for example that every word of God is flawless. We are then told later on, much like in the book of Revelation to not add to God 's words, lest we prove to be a liar. There is a request for daily bread that is arguably along the lines of the Lord's Prayer with some definite emphasis on the physical and material needs there as here.

When we transfer to different authorship in verse 10, we have some basic recommendations. We were told not to slander a servant to his master, because we will be cursed. On the subject of cursing are those who do so to their fathers and don't bless their mothers. Here we have a sexist differential in which we gather from the style of Proverbs that it is the equivalent to curse your father, as it is to not be blessing your mother. Such people actually believe that they are pure in their own minds.

Next, the author goes into comparisons of three things that are never satisfied, and then, four that never say enough. A short while after that we have the precaution of mistreating one's parents. Then there are once again three things that are too amazing for the author, but four that he does not understand. At the top of that list is the mystery of a man with a woman. This is immediately contrasted with the adulteress who eats and wipes her mouth stating she's done nothing wrong.

There are things though that nature itself cannot stand. These include a servant who becomes king, an unloved woman who is married, and a maidservant who displaces her mistress. They are an anathema to the order of nature. The chapter closes with some more reference to nature. The animal kingdom is borrowed from. There is some question if verse 28 refers to a lizard or a spider. The chapter closes with the precaution to avoid strain or anger, because that will produce strife.

Proverbs – Chapter 31

In a book that has the extolling of Lady Wisdom and the challenges of the seductress, it is quite fitting that we would close this entire book with wisdom that a king picked up from the queen mother. This mother warns the king against spending his strength on women. Alter notes that the term used is not necessarily sexual, but could refer to wealth. Closely tied to this idea of losing everything in a single event is the notion of the problems that occur from consuming excess alcohol. Alcohol, the author notes is for those who need to forget their misery. The final admonition to the king is to be a fair judge, and to defend the rights of the poor.

The book closes with an epilogue containing the traits of the wife of noble character. She is incredibly valuable. Her partner has full confidence in her because she brings him only good with no harm all the days of her life. She works from early in the morning until darkness. She is thrifty and good with business. Her lamp stays on at night, much like the parable Jesus taught in the New Testament. She reaches out to help the poor without having been told to do so. There is nothing material lacking in her household. She is clothed with both strength and dignity. She has a good sense of humor about the days to come and laughs at them. This does not imply any shortage of wisdom. This is a woman who has earned her reward of praise.

Proverbs Reflections 1-3

Once we had crossed the line to utilize some very deep resources involving exegesis on Proverbs, we decided to take a brief look at some other works. One very basic book entitled The Book of Proverbs: A Bible Study Devotional on the Wisdom of God by J. R. Heimbigner noted that this was a book with wisdom imported to us directly from God in chunk size bits for our every day life. This author felt that he could enhance that basic formula by giving us insight into his approach of devotions on Proverbs. He notes that his purpose was to understand what such wisdom means for our lives, and how to apply it and give us some jump starts from each proverb.

He quotes an ancient practice of the monks, claiming that such was the best way to receive, understand, and apply any scripture in our lives. The first principle is to do the reading. In particular, we are to read in a divine, or God like fashion. This is broken down into a four part process. Part one is to read the Bible passage. Part two is to meditate on that same passage. Part three is to pray through the passage and part four is to contemplate the passage. As such a single verse may be inspirational to fill the meditation time for the day. We are encouraged to read out loud.

One exception that we took with this author was his claim that meditation was not about emptying one's mind, but rather filling it with the passage that you are reading. As well intended as such strategy might be and even work to a fair degree, it may deprive us of an avenue of reflection that does indeed tie into the verse or scripture, but goes much beyond it. This helps to distinguish that portion of a scripture in which we do the next process of praying what God is saying about this scripture. Next, we contemplate not merely for reflection, but for application and action in our lives.

Following our source, we will comment on the particular chosen versus from each chapter in Proverbs. The first verse chosen is verse seven Proverbs chapter one. Here we read that the fear of the Lord is the beginning of knowledge, but fools despise wisdom and discipline. For this particular proverb, it may be helpful to begin at the end with the word discipline. Let us consider discipline as shaping of the individual through life events more so than a corrective action or punishment plan. Also, let us note that the fear is more of a respect process, for something beyond one's self. Also, there is an apparent distinction between the knowledge that begins with respect and the apparent knowledge, but fools have which does not involve wisdom.

The selection from chapter 2 is verse two, which tells us that turning your ear to wisdom and applying your heart to understanding, will lead eventually to understanding the fear of the Lord, and finding the knowledge of God. The preface to this is that it takes a teacher to lead us, and that we have to hunger and thirst for insight and cry out loud for understanding. We have to treat this, as though it was a valuable and buried treasure. We are reminded of the parable that Jesus describes in the New Testament about such a buried treasure, compared to the parable of the talents in which a human buries his talent in a field. Also, his admonition to hunger and thirst for righteousness.

The selection from chapter 3 is verses five and six, which read trust in the lord, with all your heart, and lean not on your own understanding but in all your ways, acknowledge him, and he will make your paths straight. The implication here is not necessarily that we are on the wrong path, but rather that we have taken an inefficient route that would benefit it from being straightened out. This does not tell us to ignore our own understanding, but rather to request the assistance from God with our heart, and not the mere intellectual knowledge of our own mind.

Proverbs Reflections 4-9

The chosen verse four chapter 4 is verse 23. There we are told above all else to guard our heart, for it is the Wellspring of life. A wellspring by definition is an original and bountiful source of something. This verse ties in to the creation story in which we are made in the image of God. In addition, this is a bountiful source, which we are to tap into. Furthermore, we are to protect that source for which we are given some information on how to do so following that. We are to keep our gaze on what is in front of us and avoid corrupt talking.

Our verse for reflection from chapter 5 is number 21. For the Lord says clearly, what a man does, examining every path he takes. There is a subtle suggestion of free will involved in this verse. God recognizes that there are many paths that humans may take. God is able to see the outcomes of those pathways not merely after they have been chosen, but also before that choice. While that choice is still ours as humans to have, we may enhance a beneficial outcome from such choice by doing the prayer requests and meditation that we mentioned earlier.

In chapter 6, the reflection echoes the sixth commandment to honor our mother and our father. We read and verse 20 through 22 my son, keep your father 's commands and do not forsake your mothers teaching. Bind them upon your heart forever. Fasten them around your neck. When you walk, they will guide you. When you sleep, they will watch over you. When you are awake, they will speak to you. Our parents serve as guides on this earth and a proxy for God. There is a constant state that occurs when we walk and all through our waking moments as well as when we sleep.

Chapter 7. Selects the passage of verse one through three. My son, keep my words and store up my commands within you. Keep my commands and you will live. Guard my teachings as the apple of your eye. Bind them on your fingers. Write them on the tablet of your heart. The metaphor and poetry here is rich. There are both visible and invisible reminders that are both essential and effective for helping to keep the commands of the teacher. We might follow up the selection with the reminder that we are to call wisdom, our sister, and that understanding is more distant kin.

In chapter 8 verse 14 we read that counsel and sound judgment are mine. I have understanding and power. We are not told directly that this is a commandment from God. Rather beginning in verse 14 we read that wisdom herself is speaking. Wisdom possesses knowledge, along with discretion, which combination helps to create wisdom. Along with this is that fear of the Lord or respect. It is also avoiding the arrogance of pride, which believes that it has some unique insight, not already known by Wisdom.

Our selection for chapter 9 is verse 10 in which we read that the fear of the lord is the beginning of wisdom, and knowledge of the Holy One is understanding. here we have the intersection of knowledge about the universal spirit, along with fear or respect of that spirit and wisdom. Fear or respect is a necessary prerequisite. However, it is only the beginning and not the end game. Nor is knowledge about God the end game. we would add that wisdom is the end game as it shows up in actionable measures in our daily life. It is not merely knowing what to do, but knowing with who, and when.

Proverbs Reflections 10-15

The verse chosen for chapter 10 of Proverbs is verse nine. This says that the man of integrity walks securely, but he who takes crooked paths will be found out. This, of course, calls to mind the ancient biblical concept of staying on the straight and narrow. It is easy to tell if someone has deviated from the straight and narrow. The man of integrity is a likened unto king David in the 23rd song in which he fears no evil, even though he is walking in the valley of the shadow of death.

The selection from chapter 11 is the second verse in which we read pride leads to disgrace, but with humility comes wisdom. We are reminded that we are still supposed to have integrity. Integrity is a guide in and of itself. Indeed, we are told a short, while later, in the chapter, that the righteousness of the upright or people of integrity does deliver them. It delivers them from evil. It keeps them on the straight and narrow referenced in the last chapter. Is not deliverance from evil a demand Jesus told us to employ in the Lord's Prayer?

The selection from chapter 12 is verse 11. We read that a hard worker has plenty of food, but a person who chases fantasies has no sense. One of the versions notes that such a person lacks judgment. To be clear we are advised at some level to have the type of judgment that is discernment. This is a strong precaution even against speculation. To be clear it is part of the universal theme throughout Proverbs of hard physical work. Later on, we say that, while our judgment often involves another individual, the prudent person keeps knowledge for themselves, or to themself.

In chapter 13 verse 11, we read that dishonest money, dwindles away, but he who gathers money little by little makes it grow. As we noted elsewhere, this is almost like a compound interest type of process. It is also in support of the western work ethic of working hard and accumulating little by little. Again, we recall the parable of the talents in which the man who had only one talent, was not chastised, because he had only one talent, but rather because he did not invest it and make more.

Verse 30 is chosen from chapter 14. There we read that a heart at peace gives life to the body, but that in the rots the bones. Some versions interpret this as being like a cancer of the bones with jealousy, etc. there is much to be said about this approach, even with modern medicine. Being at peace helps to activate the parasympathetic system, which works in concert with the sympathetic system. Unfortunately, the sympathetic nervous system or flight or fright system often goes into overdrive and produces too much cortisol and adrenaline and related hormones.

In chapter 15 verse 22 we note that plans fail for lack of counsel, but with many advisers, they succeed. There is almost the implication, that quality of the advisers takes a backseat to the quantity. We know on a logical basis that such is not the case. In real life, though this may be quite practical in which we weigh in on everyone's opinion in leadership before we go to war just as presidential councils do to this day. Perhaps, sometimes we need to listen to many different opinions before the one voice stands out. This calls to mind the first verse of this chapter in which a gentle answer turns away wrath.

Proverbs Reflections 16-21

In chapter 16 of proverbs verse 21 we read that the wise in the heart are called discerning, and that pleasant words promote instruction. That wisdom of the heart is expanded upon in the chapter. It is also a fountain of life for those who have it. It is also a guide to the words that come out of our mouths. This discernment helps us to get past the challenge of verse 25 in which we are told that there is a way that seems right to someone, but that leads to death.

Proverbs chapter 17 verse 27 tells us that a man of knowledge uses words with restraint, and a man of understanding, is even tempered. A corollary of this comes in the next verse in which we are told that a fool may even appear wise or discerning if he merely hold his tongue. In either case, actions speak louder than words. Conversely, a wise person who has discernment can listen to a rebuke, even from a fool and still apply what is meaningful for improvement in their life.

In chapter 18 verse 15 we read that the heart of the discerning acquires knowledge, and that the ears of the wise seek it out. A few verses before this, we were told that he who answers before listening is full of folly and shame. The 16th verse notes that a gift opens the way for the giver, and ushers him into the presence of the great. While, of course, there is a material connection with this we might consider the gift of listening, as opening a door to something higher than we had imagined.

The entire book of Proverbs is a book of advice. In chapter 19 verse 20 we are told to listen to advice and to accept instruction, and in the end you will be wise. To be clear wisdom is the end game. Yet in a circular fashion, it is wisdom which begins it all. In order to acquire such wisdom, we need to set apart the purposes of men. This is followed by a statement that What a man desires is unfailing love. Could we have a better definition of putting it all together than the love from God?

In chapter 20 verse five we read that the purposes of a man's heart are deep waters, but that a man of understanding draws them out. This recalls the earlier reference to deep waters. Also, we see once again that many claim to have unfailing love that we have attributed to God in the last chapter, but how can we find such a faithful person with such love? A short while later we have another rhetorical question of who can say that they have kept their heart pure and clean, like those deep waters without sin.

In chapter 21 the fifth verse is also the selection here. We are told that the plans of the diligent lead to profit as surely as haste leads to poverty. Proverbs is a practical book. This is very practical economic advice. In modern terms, if we fail to plan, then we plan to fail. We should not limit planning, or this sentence of scripture to merely economical. Planning means having a spiritual practice that is a routine. We are then cautioned to avoid the haste of the first philosophy or religious practice that catches our attention. Rather, we are to weigh in on that for the meaning of our life.

Proverbs Reflections 22-27

In Proverbs chapter 22 verse six we are given so much hoped for wisdom, that all parents of every generation wish for. There we are told to train child in the way he should go, and when he is old, he will not turn from it. This is one of those troubling verses for parents, who have indeed instructed their children, only to have them be the prodigal who never returns or reforms. Perhaps the best thing that we can see here is that the verse mentions that when that child is old that they will not depart from that instruction. It may take them a while to come around for those who eventually do, but God does not have the preoccupation with time that we do.

For a book that has much practical economic advice when we were told to buy something, there may be something worthy of our attention. Inverse 23 of chapter 23 we were told to buy the truth and not to sell it. The second part is to get wisdom, discipline, and understanding. We are told that everything has a price. This includes wisdom and truth. Perhaps this is practical advice of paying for our mentors. Perhaps it refers to the time and effort that we put into this. The close corollaries that go with this are indeed discipline with understanding.

Chapter 24 continues the theme of wisdom in verse 14. There we are told to know also, that wisdom is sweet to your soul. If you find it, there is a future hope for you and your hope will not be cut off. When we add the word also after we have used other adjective modifiers, we may get the impression that this is an afterthought, not as important as the earlier attributes of wisdom. This is not necessarily the case here. However, there is no presumption that we will find wisdom because of the word If as the second part of this verse. We were told under such circumstances that there can be a future hope. Of course all hope is in the future, but something will be better than it is at this moment. However, as the last portion implies, this hope is eternal.

Chapter 25 like much of the Original Testament had to be well-known by Jesus, along with other Jewish individuals of his era. In verse 21 we read that if your enemy is hungry, give him food to eat. If he is thirsty, give him water to drink. We see echoes of this in the parable of the sheep and the goats, in which Jesus replies with his famous statement when I was hungry you fed me, and when I was thirsty, you gave me drink, etc. The implication here is this is regardless of your belief system, your religion, or even whether or not, you are an enemy. Elsewhere we were told to bless those who persecute us by Jesus in the sermon on the mount. Indeed, Jesus merely expanded on what was given to him from measures like this proverb.

In chapter 26 verse 20 we return to some very practical advice. There were read that without wood a fire goes out. Without gossip a quarrel dies down. as is common with many of the proverbs, the first section is a set up for the second. In this case, we have the analogy, drawn and comparison of wood, essential for a fire, just as gossip is the perpetuation of a quarrel. We take it even through this proverb, that quarrels will happen. They may even happen between friends and respectful people. They are not necessarily a bad thing. However, once we introduced gossip into the equation, we are asking for perpetuation and acceleration of the quarrel.

Verse 17 is the selection from chapter 27. There we read as iron, sharpens iron, so one man sharpens another. In this regard we see that first of all, it is important to stay sharp. Secondly, it takes a like source in order to either get us to sharpness or keep us there. We might think that such is the responsibility of an opportunity of a close friend or mentor. In reality an enemy could serve the same purpose.

Proverbs Reflections 28-31

In Proverbs chapter 28 verse 20 we read that a faithful man will be richly blessed, but one eager to get rich will not go unpunished. A short, while, after that we read that a stingy man is eager to get rich, and is unaware that poverty awaits him. In a sense we see that the eagerness and stinginess to both to obtain for oneself material possessions and then keep them for oneself will not in the long run be rewarded. This is echoed in the New Testament by Jesus when he notes that the measure that we give will be the measure that we receive.

In verse 23 of chapter 29 of Proverbs we read that a man's pride brings him low, but a man of lonely spirit gains honor. The short version of the first part is that pride goes before a fall. Humility is the second part of the equation. This type of humility does not deny one's ability or responsibility. It is more of a reference to meekness or discipline as to whether one exercises for others the awareness of those abilities.

Two verses are selected from chapter 30 of Proverbs. In verses, 18 and 19, we read there are three things that are too amazing for me, for that, I do not understand: the way of an eagle in the sky, the way of a snake on a rock, the way of a ship on the highest see, and the way of a man with a maiden. Another way to frame this is that these observations are not reducible to explanations. We must not only accept them at face value, but also appreciate them for their very nature.

Chapter 31 is the concluding chapter of the book of Proverbs. It is well known for its epilogue, in which we have the wife of noble character well defined. However, there are other elements worthy of our attention, including verse eight. There we read to speak up for those who cannot speak up for themselves, for the rights of all who are destitute. This is followed by speaking up, and judging fairly and defending the rights of the poor and needy. This social responsibility and commentary absolutely is wonderfully paired with the role that women play in making it all happen.

As we conclude this section, we acknowledge our debt to the book by J.R. Heimbigner entitled The Book of Proverbs: A Bible Study Devotional on the wisdom of God. There he issued a challenge to read the scripture and meditate and then to put it in to practice. We took the liberty of using his chosen verses, although from a different translation. As we note elsewhere, we had never used any other significant resources for our earlier books as we wished the reader to be able to reach their own conclusions as we had without undue influence.

Once we felt that Proverbs was so unique we felt obliged to employ the fairly deep scholarly reflections of Fox and Alter. Frankly, these rich sources are not so readily available and might seem tedious to many readers. The work by

Heimbigner allowed us to accomplish what we sought by having basic reflections in our own way. This was refreshing given that many books still tried to connect these works strongly to King Solomon which simply cannot be justified with the information available. Also some tried to tie these books strongly to their own interpretation of the New Testament Christ. Such was not the intention of the group of writers who penned the Proverbs. Therefore, to get the most out of the original authors perspective, try to avoid that trap, no matter how appealing it might be. To do so denies the historical perspective as well as their prevailing strength.

ECCLESIASTES

INTRODUCTION

ECCLESIASTES

My devotion is a recommendation to read Ecclesiastes for a new perspective on the results of our actions on Life, Eternity, our family and our community. I used to think Ecclesiastes was a negative book-- condemning everything as Meaningless. Not so anymore. Good and Righteous behavior is presented, but often accompanied with warnings and consequences. But behavior warnings still abound, many rightly depicted as evil, "to be avoided" or meaningless, worthless effort, chasing after the wind. There are no trivial matters in Ecclesiastes. The verses In Ecclesiastes are often presented as a series of short two-line observations resulting in one of two different conclusions:

> The observation reflects a positive action or emotion
> Or a Meaningless situation

Healthy personal relationships are celebrated as well as God based community and worship activities, such as charity and prayer. Then there are the other types where human political behavior is presented as meaningless, meaningless because it has no true value for "good" in this life or eternity. These actions are self-centered, power based and ephemeral. - strictly short-term, self-gratifying actions, where God and faith and the Golden Rule are not apparent among the people or communities presented in these "meaningless" observations

My Suggestion is to Personalize Ecclesiastes

Read Ecclesiastes and record the health advisories given for personal and family community life Record the self-centered political, religious and personal situations that are "meaningless"

Realize Its Single point – worship/follow the only Reality -- God

Rich

Chapter 1

Ecclesiastes is our third book under discussion in this treatise. The author is unknown. While some circles like to think of this as written by Solomon, the evidence is overwhelming against that. This is based on careful linguistic studies and other historical items that find their way in to the work. This is not to say that the author did not wish for that perception of the connection with Solomon to be present. Indeed likely, there was the interest in having a high degree of wisdom attached to this such as was reputed to be the case with Solomon. In this regard it is much like Proverbs.

Alter tells us that the meaning of Ecclesiastes may be to assemble. Even more so this Hebrew verb form applies only to humans as the objects suggesting that it might reflect an assembly of people. It is one of the newer books in the Original Testament. The poetic author who was sometimes dialectic well before Hegel, has no respect for time, history, politics, or much else of human concern. Alter argues that for all of the problems of the King James Version, that it comes the closest in meaning of the English texts. He further notes that the work has the preoccupation with items that move but can't be seen or grasped. Think of the wind. Much like the whirlwind in Job, the wind in Ecclesiastes serves as the appropriate symbol for understanding.

The poetry of this work, perhaps here outshines wisdom. Indeed, we should be cautious about ascribing too much wisdom to this work merely because it is included in the Bible. It is indeed conceivable that it was largely included in the Biblical canon because of the theoretical connection with Solomon. The famous poetry, in chapter 3 has worked its way into speeches, including ones that I have given and songs, including those sung at my own wedding. For our purposes, here we will refer to the wisdom books by Robert Alter and some of his citations, including Michael Fox.

After the introduction that these are the words of the teacher, son of David king in Jerusalem, we have various translations that it is meaningless or it is absurd or the like. The usage of the term son of David does not imply that there was a clear connection with Solomon but was rather a technique to emphasize connections with important people. Here the author asks what does a person gain from all of the labor and all of their toiling. After all the generations will come and go, although the sun and earth and wind, and other elements will endure.

Alter points out the difficulty of translating this first true statement. Some have rendered it as meaningless but perhaps the term absurd comes closer. It is the type of absurdity that the Danish existentialist Soren Kierkegaard discloses in his works. Of course, there may be meaning, but it is not in the conventional measures that we consider. It is not in the perpetuation of the species, or even the lineage of David, which he hoped so much for. This is illustrated in the third verse, along with the fourth verse in which we are asked what a person gains from all their labor when generations come and go.

In chapter one the author points out that the true creation remains forever. Humans, meanwhile, are not able to create anything new, as we are told in verse 10 of the first chapter. If someone tries to label something as new, we will be reminded that it was already present long ago. All our senses, including the eyes. can never see all of nature. Nor can the ear ever hear all of nature.

Even the type of wisdom that a king who has sought wisdom can gain much knowledge, and even a wise reputation, will recognize in the long run, that it is madness and folly, and the chasing after the wind. After all, with much wisdom comes much sorrow, and with more knowledge there comes grief. There is at times almost a Zen or even Taoist tone to some of the sayings. Consider chapter 1 verse 15 whatever is twisted cannot be straightened, what is lacking cannot be counted.

Chapter 2

We recall the closing of chapter 1 with its almost Taoist perspective. For with much wisdom comes much sorrow; The more knowledge, the more grief. With this we recall the middle age philosopher who at the dawn of the scientific age noted that knowledge would increase while wisdom diminished. Perhaps the grief associated with the splitting of the atom is inherent in this process.

With the start of chapter 2, we are given a subtle approach and new twist. With the opening verse the author notes that he thought in his heart. This is above and beyond the mere mental thinking that we experienced in the first chapter. Indeed the author then moves quickly to total body thinking and experience by exploring pleasure to find out what is good. Normally we might think that what is good is meaningful or that even something meaningful is more important than something good.

Whatever our perspective on that issue, the author is about to settle that score. He raises the rhetorical question of what pleasure actually accomplishes. He tried the usual measures, including wine and embracing folly. To be sure, he still knows that he was go by wisdom through this time, perhaps he has even been given some insight to weigh in on these measures. He next undertook great projects of architecture, and planting with gardens and parks. He even provided reservoirs as a sort of conservation project to help trees and plants flourish.

Long before we so-called moderns thought of our lofty notions to save the Earth, whether a species that is threatened or from global warming, the author pointed out that you will not necessarily get the meaning that you are looking for by such actions. He then turned to the accumulation of possessions of silver and gold, as well as the commodity of the day with herds and flocks. He knows that he had male and female slaves. He had male and female singers. This did not bring him the meaning that he sought.

He goes on to note that he did not deny himself anything that his eyes desire, nor any pleasure conceived in his heart. However, even having a harem did not bring him what others might have thought was pleasure and meaning. Yet strangely, in the second part of verse 10, he knows that his heart did take delight in his efforts, and that such a delight was apparently the only reward for all his toil. He then goes on to qualify that everything that he had accomplished and toiled for was meaningless.

In fact, he uses the statement that everything was a chasing after the wind. Shortly, there after he does recognize that wisdom is better than folly just as light is better than darkness. Nonetheless, the same fate will be for both the wise and the fool. He knows that both will not only die, but that both will be forgotten. If this is supposed to represent king Solomon as the son of David, then it is a major slap in the face to David, who was always preoccupied with the perpetuation of his knowledge and kingdom.

Chapter 2 & 3

At the conclusion of chapter 2 in Ecclesiastes, we see that the author actually ends up stating that he hated life. The reason that he gives is that the work that he did was grievous to him. More specifically it was meaningless, and a chasing after the wind, which phrase he likes to repeat. He then says specifically that he did not wish to toil so hard to leave behind measures for someone who came after him. This is in contradistinction to David, who wanted to leave a legacy and a kingdom for his family forever without necessarily giving them anything to go on.

The author seems to favor and prefigure the so-called western work ethic that you must toil for your own successes, as opposed to reaping what you did not sow. He knows that all work is grief and pain whether day or night. The best that someone can hope for he knows is to eat drink and find satisfaction in your own work. he believes this to be ordained by the hand of God. Furthermore, he questions whether anyone could appreciate such measures without the hand of God. Then he makes the curious distinction that God gives wisdom and knowledge and happiness to the person who pleases him, but to the sinner he gives the exact task that the author did not like, namely of storing up wealth for the sake of someone else.

All of this is a wonderful background to the very poetic chapter 3, especially the first eight verses. There the author notes that there is a time for everything under the heavens, whether it is being born or dying, or planting or uprooting, or killing or healing, and so on down the line. He even knows that there's a time to hate as well as a time for war and a time for peace. He also knows that there is a time for love, but arguably never gets around to defining what that might be.

Then, after this wonderful recognition of a time for everything, the author asks what any worker gains from their toil. He also knows that God has placed a burden on the entire human race. Then he returns to the theme that everything is beautiful and its own time. He declares that the concept of eternity was something that God placed upon the human heart. God is meanwhile, of course, aloof to time in any sense. He then notes another gift from God would be to be able to eat and drink and find satisfaction in one's work.

The author wishes to be a clear that God will call to judgment, not only the wicked, but the righteous for every activity, and every deed that they have ever performed. He then goes on to some self reflection, projecting that God test humans. In the long run human beings will have the same fate as the animals which the author also sees as meaningless. He closes with the statement that there's nothing better for a person to do than to enjoy their work.

Chapter 4

The wonderfully poetic chapter 3 of Ecclesiastes starts with a time for everything under the heavens. Chapter 4 in contradistinction talks about things under the sun, and all of the oppression that is visible under the sun. People that are oppressed have no comforter. The author goes on to declare that people who are dead are happier than the living, though one wonders where he would wo have derived such conclusion. However, better still is the person who has never been born, as though such a person could actually exist, and not exist simultaneously.

He then relates that all achievement arises from a persons envy of someone else. This, too is meaningless and a chasing after the wind. If it was possible, he would favor having a mere handful of tranquility, than two handfuls of toil and chasing after the wind. In earlier chapters, there is a lament about leaving the fruits of one's labor to even your own offspring. Now in this chapter, he pities the person who has neither son or brother to live the results of his toil to.

Then, towards the end of this chapter, the author makes the statement that it is better to be a poor and wise youth, than an old and foolish king, who no longer knows how to heed a warning. There is the suggestion that even such a youth coming from prison to the kingship, or from poverty to such might have done all right because of that. And yet even such a successor to the king ends up, not being pleasing in the long run. Therefore, this too, is meaningless and a chasing after the wind.

Chapter 5

The author opens this chapter with the admonition to guard both your steps into the house of God, as well as your mouth, and to not be hasty. Yet shortly thereafter he instructs people to not delay in fulfilling their vows to God. He suggests that it is better not to make a vow, then to make one and not fulfill it. In addition to too many words, he gives precaution to too much dreaming. However, he feels that there is significant benefit in fearing God.

The author continues the theme that all toil is meaningless, because someone else may get the benefit, including the king. By the same token, whoever loves money never has enough. This, too, is meaningless. Aft all, if a persons goods happen to increase, so too do those who consume them. Meanwhile, paradoxically the rich do not get adequate sleep because of their abundance compared to a regular laborer who has sweet sleep. Then the author echoes the words of Job basically saying naked have I come from my mothers womb, and naked will I return.

To conclude this chapter, the author nones notes what he considers to be good. He basically says that you may as well enjoy your toil or some labor under the sun in order to eat and drink and find satisfaction. After all, you only have a few days so to speak to do this. If you happen to be one of those who is blessed with wealth and possessions, then, your ability to enjoy such is a gift from God to be respected. Strangely such satisfied individuals have a gladness of heart that keeps them from reflecting on the days of their life.

Chapter 6

In this chapter, the author describes that God participates in evil. This evil ways heavily upon humans. After all, God, give us people, possessions and honor, and wealth, and everything that their hearts desire. However, the same God does not grant him the ability to enjoy them, and therefore the fruits of their toil are left for strangers to enjoy. This is considered not only meaningless, but a grievous evil. If we are to take this book seriously we must not neglect the fact that this evil is attached to God.

Indirectly, the author takes a stab at David himself when he says in verse three of chapter 6, that a man can have 100 children and live many years, but if you cannot enjoy his prosperity, then a stillborn child is better off than he. Given that David was obsessed with the forever clause through his offspring, this is somewhat of an indirect jab at him. The author also knows that a proper burial is essential for a meaningful life although this irony is not explained. However, a stillborn is better off than such an individual.

The author notes that we toil to satisfy our appetite, and yet it never is satisfied. In this sense, the wise individuals do not have a clear advantage over fools. The author notes that it is better to see something then to have the appetite roving. Of course, this metaphor could be applied to many measures in life. He goes on to note that humans are really not going to come up with anything new that they can name because everything that can be known has already been known. Furthermore, the more words that are utilized, the less than meaning. Once again, all of this is chasing after wind.

Chapter 7

In this chapter, the author will turn some things on their head. The opening statement seems usually understood on its first reading in that a good name is better than fine perfume. Although there's nothing really profound about that, the point here is that a good name does appear to count for something. However, the author then steps into the position in the same verse that the day of death is better than the day of birth. This is not derived from a perspective of going to heaven because the author did not have such a perspective.

He then goes on to note that a house of mourning is better than a house of feasting, and that death is the destiny of everyone which the living should take to heart. Perhaps our Taoist friends can add some perspective here along with those from the Zen tradition and illustrate how the removal of measures helps to unclutter the mind and focus on the moment. Then we get into paradoxes where the author notes that frustration is better than laughter because a sad face is good for the heart. Those of us caught up in the pursuit of happiness might do well to pause and reflect on this.

Next, we find ourselves dealing with proverb like measures. The heart of the fool is in the house of pleasure. Better to heed the rebuke of the wise than to listen to the song of fools. Extortion turns a wise person into a fool. The end of a matter is better than the beginning. Patience is better than pride. Anger resides in the lap of fools. We are warned about suggesting that the good old days were better than now. Wisdom is like an inheritance and is a good thing.

A statement of reflection is that wisdom preserves those who have knowledge. Then we have another Zen moment where the author notes that success is the same as failure because God made them both. This is tied with a therefore clause in that the good and bad outcomes prevent people from discovering their future. Yet the fact that the righteous perish in their righteousness is meaningless just as is the wicked living long in their wickedness. The we are told that we would do well to not be overwise or overwicked, as though it might be ok to be a little wicked.

We are told here that God is a God of the center because God avoids all extremes. Yet immediately after this we are told that who is there who is righteous and has not sinned. Next we have some practical advice about not eavesdropping because we might hear our subordinates cursing us. Then a statement labeled profound by the author with which we concur: whatever exists is far off and most profound. He then closes the chapter noting that God created man upright, but that only one in a thousand stays that way. According to the author, there is not even a single woman.

Chapter 8

In the first verse of chapter 8, we see a statement that a person's wisdom brightens their face and changes its hard appearance. Perhaps this is because there is a comfort zone that is exhibited with one feels wisdom, in that there is also peace and calm. No one is quite like anyone who has wisdom, and with that an explanation. This explanation appears to go beyond that of mere knowledge. In fact, it may even be a quiet acceptance of profound measures that are otherwise inexplicable.

Immediately after this profound expression, we have some echoes of David. In verse two we are told to obey the kings come in because you took an oath before God. David was quite adept at pairing up responsibility to the king and God and will always have in mind what was in it for himself. With the same concept, we are noted to not be in a hurry to leave the kings presence, or to stand up for a bad cause, because after all the king will do whatever he pleases. Who after all can say to a king what are you doing?

The author continues to tie into this Davidic way of thinking by noting that whoever obeys the kings command will come to no harm, and that the wise heart will know the proper time and procedure. He then echoes his own much longer chapter 3 note in regards to the time and place for everything by repeating that there is a proper time and procedure for every matter. In this simple verse, though we have the inclusion of procedure has been an essential part of the equation in addition to the time.

He then takes a shot about speculation about the future. This again is somewhat analogous to a Zen like moment of focusing on the now, perhaps. However, it may be equally a potshot about his possible connection to David, who is always preoccupied with the future. Perhaps even prophets might be in this category because the author notes that no one can tell someone else what is to come. By the same token, no one has the power over the time of their death. Wickedness, meanwhile, will not release those who practice it just as those who are engaged in the time of war cannot be discharged.

The author has also perhaps, learned another negative lesson from David when he says in verse nine that there is a time when a man lords it over others to his own hurt. Certainly in our book entitled David and Michelangelo, we see strong evidence for such action. This is followed by the perspective that even the wicked when buried may receive praise in the city in which they did their evil actions. Perhaps this is meant to tie in closely to the next verse, in which, if a sentence for a crime is not quickly carried out, then people are filled with evil schemes.

In the long run, though, the author knows that it is still better with those who fear God and revere him. The wicked will ultimately pay a price for not fearing God. This statement and concept is juxtaposed with something immediately following which contradicts this. He notes that the righteous get what the wicked deserved and the wicked get what the righteous deserve. When this happens, it is meaningless. Therefore, you might as well enjoy your life because there's nothing better under the sun and eat drink and be glad. This is what will give people ultimate joy. Still, the author concludes that no one can figure out the meaning of life.

Chapter 9

A profound statement is one that we recognize we may not fully appreciate at the time, but perhaps with further reflection and time might be able to do so. A bizarre statement is one that we feel that we will never be able to make any sense out of and not because of our own limitations, but because of the absurdity of the statement. if we are being honest the book of Ecclesiastes has some of each. Perhaps chapter 9 as much as any.

In the opening verse and chapter 9, the author concludes that the righteous and the wise and their actions are in God's hands. Despite this, though no one knows where their love or hate awaits them. This may include not only the wise, but the wicked and not so wise. After all, everyone shares a common destiny whether the righteous or wicked or clean or unclean or those who offer sacrifices or those who do not. The author calls this the great evil, and that the same destiny overtakes everyone regardless of their actions.

We have a hard time reconciling the next portion which says that the hearts of people are full of evil with madness in their hearts while they live, and then they join the dead. So far so good but right after that, he says that anyone who is among the living has hope because after all a live dog is better off than a dead lion. It is hard to reconcile this with a statement from earlier chapters in which it is better to be a stillborn, and to have never have lived. Once again, living people are destined to know they will die, but the dead, of course know nothing.

The author precludes any notion of eternal life or heaven, noting that the dead have no further reward, and even their name is forgotten. All emotions whether love or hate, and jealousy are vanished after they die. Somehow the conclusion to all of this is to go and eat your food in gladness and drink your wine with a joyful heart because God has already approved what you do. This derives from the fact that God has blessed all things as good. The author even admonishes us to anoint ourselves and to be clothed in pure white.

As much as the author uses the statement of meaningless life, we can be fairly certain that he really means it when he uses the same phrase twice in the same sentence. This is exactly what happens in verse nine in which he says that you are to enjoy life with your wife, whom you love all the days of your meaningless life that God has given you under the sun and your meaningless days. It is difficult to make an argument for Solomon with all of his wives being the author of this particular chapter whatever else we can construe about the rest of the book.

In addition, we see a prefiguring of the myth of Sisyphus before the Greeks told the story, and before Albert Camus wrote the story by the same name. In that myth, Sisyphus is condemned to repeat his actions perpetually without achieving the goal. The existentialists argues that the work its self is the goal. They may even go so far as to say that the only meaning that can be derived from the absurdity of not reaching a goal is to do the task that we seem to have been given without regard for the end result.

A few verses later, he notes that it is not skill or strategy or brilliance that determines outcomes, but rather time and chance. Malcolm Gladwell outline this nicely in his book Outliers. The author concludes that wisdom is better than weapons, and that quiet words of the wise are more to be heeded than the shouts of a ruler of fools. However, right before that, he notes the story of a poor man who is wise, who once saved the city by his wisdom, but was forgotten. He notes that even though wisdom is better than strength that that poor man's wisdom is despised

Chapter 10

When literature is filled with ambiguity or unfamiliarity, it is easy to read into something that you would particularly like to see. Chapter 10 compares dead flies, giving perfume a bad smell with folly outweighing wisdom and honor. Then we see something that some political parties would like to see in writing in which the heart of the wise inclines to the right but the heart of the fool to the left. Foolish people tend to show how stupid they are, even when they go walking.

The author, then turns to practical advice of not getting particularly disturbed about a rulers anger against yourself, because calmness could lay great offenses to rest. Then he points out that those same rulers create an evil when they please fools in high positions. They also suggest that the rich people should occupy these positions and not the low ones. Perhaps this is a political statement, chapter after all.

He then notes the irony that those who dig a pit might fall into it, and that whoever takes stones from a quarry might be injured from them, or that the person who splits logs may be endangered by them. Next, he slaps some humor into a deadly serious statement in which, if the snake bites the charmer before it is charmed, then the charmer receives no fee.

Once again, in this book, the author distinguishes himself from David. He knows that blessed is the land whose king is of noble birth, and woe to the land whose king was a servant, which would've certainly been applicable to David. Then he notes the proverb that because of idle hands that the house leaks. We can certainly live with the statement that a feast is made for laughter and that wine makes life merry. Yet how do we draw the conclusion from that same verse 19 and which we are told that money is the answer for everything?

Chapter 11

This chapter is full of Proverbs without profundity. The one possible exception is the perpetual reference to the wind. This time it occurs with the twist that whoever watches the wind will not plant. How do you actually watch the wind? Although we are admonished to plant our seed in the morning, we were told not to let our hands be idle at night, because we never know what will succeed. Then in direct contradistinction to earlier statements in earlier chapters he knows that however many years anyone may live, let them enjoy them all.

Chapter 12

In an earlier chapter, we noted the frequent use of the word meaningless throughout this short work. We also noted that when it occurs twice in the same sentence or verse that it is to be strongly heeded. If such is the case, then as we wrap up this book, we would do well to look at a verse that has the word meaningless in it three times which is exactly what happens in verse eight of chapter 12. This comes after statements, like remembering your creator in your youth, before troubles come. He then goes on to list a series of those troubles that befall people. Indeed, we are told to remember God before the dust returns to the ground from which it came, and the spirit returns to God, who gave it.

The conclusion of chapter 12, and the entire book of Ecclesiastes sounds a little bit disingenuous. It suggests that the teacher who wrote this was wise and imported knowledge to the people which, apparently not every wise person could do. He gave the people many proverbs and such, long and hard to find just the right words. we are warned like other books of the Bible to not add anything to these words. After all of the making of many books, there is no end and too much study wearies the body. The final statement by the author is to fear God, and keep his commandments as this is the duty of humans, because God will bring every deed into judgment whether hidden, or whether good or evil.

What Is Not Meaningless Or Absurd In The Book Of Ecclesiastes

It is certainly easy for someone to come away from a reading of the book of Ecclesiastes with despair about the meaningless of life. In fact, the title of the first chapter is that everything is meaningless. The title of the second chapter is that pleasures are meaningless. What does that leave that might have meaning in it? Perhaps we have to use the negative of the negative to come up with what may be positive in all of this.

In the first chapter, we are told that there is nothing new under the sun. Perhaps this is viewed by many as a negative but perhaps it is an extremely comforting proposition to know that, for all of our efforts, we cannot create anything of significance that is truly new. Before chapter 1 is finished we see that even wisdom that was sought seems to be meaningless. Perhaps there is the implication that not chasing for something like the wind, but letting it be, or letting it come to us is truly wisdom.

In chapter 2 verse 24 we come to the apex that cannot be beat. That is to eat drink and be happy in one's work. There is a corollary of recognizing that the gift of work and enjoyment comes from God. Those who do not have wisdom, and knowledge and happiness are destined to accumulate material possessions only to give them to other people that they may actually never know. Chapter 3 has the classic time for everything under the sun poetry. The beauty of this is that there is a time for everything including opposites in the same verse, and the same person and the same time.

In chapter 4, we see that tranquility may have meaning even more than the positive reference to work mentioned earlier. We also see that unity is better than separation in verse nine of chapter 4. In chapter 5 we see that hard work is rewarded by good sleep. Once again in this chapter, we see that it is good to eat and drink and find satisfaction in one's work which has been God given. In chapter 7, we see the value of a good name as well as the value of mourning. this chapter also talks about the benefit of being rebuked by someone who is wise. Chapter 7 notes that wisdom is a good thing like inheritance which gives credence to 2 measures being meaningful. We also recognize that it is wisdom to not pay attention to everything that people say as chapter 7 advises but strangely the converse of being selective may be a little bit harder.

In chapter 9 verse 9, we see that enjoying life with a partner that we love seems to provide benefit in an otherwise meaningless life. In that same chapter, we see that wisdom is truly better than both folly and strength. while we are told that no one knows when their hour will come, this may actually be a good thing to not know. This chapter also notes, the benefit of wisdom being better than war. in chapter 10, we see the potential benefits of noble birth, along with all things, money.

In chapter 11 we see that it is meaningful once again to work. We also see some benefit of giving away bread because it will return to us. We see the benefit of reaping what we sow. We are also told to enjoy our life no matter how long we live. Amidst all of this, we are challenged to be happy while we are young and have joy in our heart. There seems to be a distinction between bodily pleasures and those of the heart and soul. The concluding chapter 12 gives meaning to remembering our creator in our youth before trouble comes. We also see in the concluding chapter that searching for and utilizing the right words is meaningful and provides an opportunity for what one has learned to be imparted to others as verse 9 notes. Finally, we are instructed to fear God and to keep his commandments.

ECCLESIASTES AND EXISTENTIALISM

The existentialist might claim that there is not much of a thread of existentialism in the book of Ecclesiastes. Let's consider the fundamental definition of existentialism that existence precedes essence. If we take this as our working premise, then we are likely to find that well before Kierkegaard was given credit for introducing existentialism that the author of Ecclesiastes had these concepts in mind. Our linguistics may get in the way because commonly accepted phrases used in Ecclesiastes do not adequately represent the meaning.

Indeed, some have translated the concept of meaningless, which occurs in multiple settings in the book of Ecclesiastes to more properly the notion of absurdity. When this is the case, we now have a strong connection with the existentialist Albert Camus, who talked repeatedly about the absurd. The ultimate metaphor or symbol noted in the book of Ecclesiastes is chasing after the wind, which phrase is used repeatedly. This concept of may as well catch the wind was captured in the song by the same title by the folk ballad singer Donovan.

Indeed, what the author of Ecclesiastes seems to be noting was that the measures that stood for the essence of humankind at that point such as possessions and riches, and knowledge really did not seem to provide meaning for humankind. Indeed, this process is what is labeled as absurd in the sense that one works and toils all their life only to pass it on to someone else. At times the term evil is employed to describe this absurdity. The author even goes so far as to say that this is the greatest evil known to humankind.

The author of Ecclesiastes would not only go along with the notion that you can't take it with you, but further than that there was nowhere to take it. The author of Ecclesiastes does not have a concept of heaven. In this sense he parallels much of the writings of the modern existentialists who would note that discussions of heaven do not serve any purpose for improving humankind, and the misery that is attached to that. For the author of Ecclesiastes, the focus on the future, whether it would include a heaven, or simply life on this earth is absurd.

Let's examine some of the basic tenants of existentialism. Some of these key fundamentals include freedom and especially the freedom to make a choice as well as responsibility. Existentialism also seeks to address anxiety by dealing with life's changes. There is a strong emphasis on the individual. Many of these themes are evident in the book of Ecclesiastes. Towards the conclusion of Ecclesiastes, in chapter 11, we are told in verse 10 to banish anxiety from our hearts, and to cast off the troubles of our bodies. Youth and energy are overrated, especially without the conscious decision of making a contribution to something larger than One's self.

Existentialism recognizes with Ecclesiastes one does have a choice and how they move and encourages responsibility.

Both recognize that simply working for the mere sake of working and accumulating possessions does not lead to satisfaction. Ultimately Ecclesiastes notes that it is important to do the task that we are assigned, but that we are to eat drink and be merry as we were told repeatedly throughout the book, including chapters 2 and three and nine. One is encouraged to do their duty and recognize that there is a force above them. The fact that Ecclesiastes talks about the king or even God in this role is not counter to that of the existentialists who points out that ultimately one is responsible for their own happiness and well-being.

THE NOT SO GLORIOUS
TRANSFER OF POWER

Many, if not, most people are interested in having at least some wisdom to make appropriate choices and to avoid harmful decisions. If you were such a person, seeking wisdom, when would you do that? Would you do that after you had made some bad decisions? Would you do that when you had some difficult measures coming up in your life? Would you do that after you had seen somebody, you admired make reasonable decisions because they had wisdom? Would you pray for wisdom after you saw somebody whom you otherwise admired makes some decisions that may not have been so wise?

For the answers to these questions, let us turned to the book of first kings, and examine the first three chapters. A quick rundown of this will show that this is the end of the life of king David and therefore, of course of his kingship. Accordingly, there will need to be a transfer of power. Much like the movie, The King's Speech this transfer may happen while the king is still alive. Typically, under such circumstances, the king or his advisers, sense that the end is near for the effectiveness or life of such a king. How did the advisors and counsel of the court of King David come to this conclusion? This is all contained in the first chapter of First Kings where we read that King David was old and well advanced in years and could not keep warm even when the covers were placed on him. If you were a group or part of a group of advisors to King David, what would you do under the circumstances? There is a fair chance that you would ask yourself what David was noted for and what motivated him. You would want to get his mojo back. Recall our discussion from the book David and Michaelangelo in which we note that the key reason or at least one of the key reasons that David fought Goliath was not because God inspired him to do so, but rather that there was a reward involved. The reward that seemed to interest David the most was a woman, and in particular, the king's daughter.

Never mind how that turned out with the first daughter or even the second one that he ultimately abandoned after she saved his life. The point is that David's advisors recognize that David has been motivated all of his adult life by women. They may be the wife of another such as Abigail or Bathsheba. They are often known for their beauty. In recognition of this, at the end of the life of David advisors look to restore the last mojo of David. They look for a beautiful young virgin to lie beside him. They are not naïve. There is awareness, and there are expectations. However, even with these reasonable expectations, David is not up to sleeping with this beautiful young woman.

This is the strongest signal that the end is near. Indeed, after the failure to consummate the relationship with the young woman, the very next verse recognizes that the time has come for David to be replaced. In that verse one of David 's sons, Adonijah will stake his claim to the throne. He will temporarily or momentarily be king until one of the important women that David had adultery with gets word of this. No doubt she was aware of the woman sleeping with her husband. However, when queen Bathsheba hears about the son taking over for king David, instead of her own son Solomon, she orchestrates her moves to reverse this. We have detailed this elsewhere in our book David And Michaelangelo.

SOLOMON AND WISDOM

After Solomon is established as the rightful king, with the help of the right clergy, and his mother, queen Bathsheba, we get the final days of the life of David. They are filled with a horrific vengeance on people from events far earlier in his life. Such is the case of one of his former generals, who was popular and himself, crushed an uprising against one of the other sons. Also included is the poor man who taunted David, and was let go at the moment, only to be killed by the instructions of David given at the end of the life of David. We do not see in these vengeful statements and commands by the dying King David, to seek wisdom for his son who is to be king Solomon. No, rather David, dies with vengeance as his motive.

There is no death scene with father to son advice about what to do or to avoid making some of the mistakes that David did. What we have in the early kingship of Solomon is the following. He will have one of David's key generals put to death. This was a dying request from his father David. He will have someone who insulted David years earlier put to death. He will have the brother who lead the charge to take over the kingship from David put to death not because of that fact, but rather, for the fact that he wish to consummate the relationship with the beautiful woman that king David was unable to do. Now we can move on to the next chapter. King Solomon will take the daughter of an Egyptian pharaoh somewhat in turn about from the story we find from the experience of Abraham and Isaac at an earlier time in Genesis.

It is only at this time in chapter 3 of first Kings that it is finally time for King Solomon to ask for wisdom. Apparently, he did not need any wisdom to put key people to death who were associated with his father, including family. He already had an example in that in his father, and he could follow that. Apparently he did not need wisdom to marry, the daughter of a king. He already had plenty of examples again from his father, David who enjoyed beautiful women of high status, married or otherwise. No, we maintain that Solomon asked for wisdom because he saw that David really did not have it and that ending your life with vengeance was not a particularly wise thing to do as it showed a tremendous lack of forgiveness with all its toxic consequences. These are the circumstances of the wisdom seeking Solomon as the prelude to that acquisition. What is his first application of that wisdom? It's all right there in the third chapter of first kings. King Solomon will settle a dispute between two prostitutes. He will not judge them for their prostitution, but rather will recognize one of the prostitute's legitimate rights to her baby, however that baby was conceived. Now, perhaps we have wisdom.

SOLOMON'S FIRST DECISION
AFTER WISDOM

We have already reviewed at link of the timing of the acquisition of Solomons wisdom. It would appear that Solomon
felt the need for wisdom, after carrying out the vengeance
acts on behalf of his father king David, who was full of vitriolic retribution for people who had been associated with
him. Solomon proceeds to carry out those violent acts of
killing. Then he marries the daughter of a foreign king.
Now, perhaps he can have sweet dreams. Indeed, he has a
dream in which God comes to him in that dream, and asks
Solomon what he would desire. Solomon may not yet be
wise but he is also no dummy.

A dream, of course, is reflection of the subconscious.
Perhaps before he went to bed the night before his dream,
Solomon was legitimately concerned about having night-
mares given the acts of vengeance that he had performed
just because his father King David could not come to
terms with some measures himself at the end of his life.
Nonetheless, Solomon has a dream in which he senses God
coming to him and asking Solomon what it was that he
desired most. We maintain the Solomon saw that he needed
more wisdom than his spiteful father king David, in order
to govern people. Perhaps, after having his own brother put
to death, King Solomon thought that there might be a bet-

ter way. Perhaps he realized that marrying a rich beautiful woman like his father had done with the queen Bathsheba, his mother, was not enough for him even though Solomon had already had that marriage already before his wisdom.

So in his dream Solomon is, indeed granted the wisdom and discernment that he was seeking. He gets a bonus of riches and a long life because of his request. Of course, wisdom is not useful unless it is put to the test. That is what the rest of chapter 3 in first Kings is about. What better test of wisdom could we have than being approached by two unwed mothers about a property dispute. Did we mention that they were prostitutes? Did we mention that the property dispute was about a baby.

The story is all right there in chapter 3 of first Kings. Both of these unwind mothers were living together perhaps out of convenience for the prostitution work. Both of them became pregnant around the same time. Might even have been the same man which would promote more easily the potential for the bizarre forthcoming baby swap. After a few days, one of the mother's baby died after she slept on it. Apparently they did not have all the information about SIDS that was available to watch these days. That mother takes the infant from the other mother in that fateful night, and puts the dead baby under the other mother's side. The following morning, the change is discovered. The woman whose baby is still alive understandably very much wishes to have her baby back and appeals to King Solomon.

Let's look at his wisdom and judgment in this case. First of all, he does not judge the women because of their profession of prostitution. Secondly, he does not judge them for being unwed mothers. He does not judge the mother who killed her baby, figuring that this could be a legitimate action on her part without knowing that much about SIDS. No, rather his first major decision after his acquisition of wisdom is to have the baby killed. Better yet he will do it himself with a sword, and makes that command. Now at this point, both of the women probably know that Solomon has just recently killed people for grievances years ago, and killed, famous and popular generals, and killed his own brother. They have to believe he is serious about this. So do we.

We cannot make simple assumptions that Solomon knew what the outcome would be with one woman that the other rightful mother could have the baby. That is only obvious to us, in hindsight. When we reflect on the first major decision after his acquisition of wisdom, and the only decision in that first chapter of his wisdom, we perhaps can learn some valuable lessons. Perhaps it is wise for us not to judge people for their profession. Perhaps it is wise for us not to judge those who are unwed mothers. Perhaps some leniency is best when even major accidents happen. Perhaps we, too, should pray for wisdom, when we have been asked to do acts of violence on the behalf of others. Perhaps we, too, should pray for wisdom, when we have performed such acts of violence.

CONCLUSION

If we were to compare the book of Psalms with the 10 Commandments, we might suggest that the 10 Commandments are a blueprint for how we should live our lives. Meanwhile, the Psalms are a penetrating exposé of having lived. Whether it is David, who has written a Psalm or someone speaking in his voice, much of the concept is laid out in brutal and honest and unapologetic prose. David shows the range of human emotion and human living from the highs to the lows. If he were seeking a medical diagnosis, he might choose bipolar illness.

When we turn to Proverbs, we actually get some blueprint for living. This is clearly written by an author who has lived, and who recognizes whether from his own or from others the mistakes that lead to ruin. There are indeed two ways in many of the couplets at achieving a healthy and balanced life. On the one hand, there is the positive side of this is what happens for your betterment when you behave in such a way. On the other hand, here is what happens if you choose the alternative course.

Ecclesiastes can be a challenge to find meaning as we have noted in our article on existentialism and the other essay on meaningless versus meaning in the book of Ecclesiastes. What is very clear is that much of our striving is meaningless. This includes striving for material possessions and to some degree even the western ethic of hard work. To some degree, and in an indirect fashion, we are given a challenge to accept life and go with the flow. This type of yielding is seen in the Chinese Way of the Tao.

We might return to the 10 Commandments and see if there is fulfillment in the book of Psalms or Proverbs or Ecclesiastes. Certainly, we can see reference to the challenges of serving other gods and idols as referenced in the 10 Commandments when we read the book of Psalms. When we are admonished to not take the name of the Lord God in vain, we have to feel that for all of his faults that David does make an honest appeal to the Lord God, even in his woe is me laments.

We do not see much reference to keeping the sabbath day holy in these works. For all the wisdom and personal exposure that is given by bearing heart and soul, we do not see much reference to honoring the parents. David does not mention his earthly father and rarely mentions his mother. Indeed, in our book, David and Michelangelo, we note a deviation for most of the 10 Commandments in the Bathsheba affair alone whether it was the murder, adultery, stealing or bearing false witness, or coveting as in the last five commandments.

Ultimately, we recognize that motive matters. This seems to be the intention of the original 10 Commandments. We have written on this elsewhere about how natural even in today's world it is to covet what our neighbor has and to think murderous thoughts or adulterous thoughts of desire. The commandments are there because such actions and thoughts are indeed inherent in the life of humankind.

David is the ultimate manifestation of such thinking and action.

If we consider psalm number 119 as a summary of his life, we may see, perhaps a glimmer of hope, not only for David but as well for ourselves. There in closing verses we see longing for salvation by following the law. There is praise and recognition for the law. There is the recognition that he is strayed like a lost sheep and wishes to be found as a servant much like the story of the one last sheep, that Jesus referenced, perhaps with David and this Psalm in mind in his New Testament analogy of the one last sheep

Ultimately, we wish to believe that David provided a survival guide for us through his work in the Psalms, even if such survival guide occurs in a few scant verses. Like the couplets in Proverbs, though with much longer intervals between the correct path and the incorrect, David shows us the consequences for survival when he chooses the negative. Certainly, his frustrations and frailties depicted there parallel the stories related in Samuel and First Kings.

David, like us, can only survive his many ordeals by seeking God and wanting to be treated the way a farmer would seek a solitary lost sheep. Proverbs presents couplets with choice for survival or disaster depending on the choice of our pathway. By questioning much of hat is considered desirable, Ecclesiastes offers us the notion that our mere existence is an important element in survival even if our choices often seem meaningless. When we subject everything under the sun to scrutiny and questioning we will find a way to survive what seems overwhelming.